BUFFALO I

by Sun Bear

**A NATIVE AMERICAN'S VIEW
OF HIS CULTURE, RELIGION AND HISTORY**

**Cover design and painting by Nimimosha
Photographs by courtesy of the Smithsonian Institution,
Washington, D. C.**

First Bear Tribe Edition, 1976
Second Bear Tribe Edition, 1978
Third Bear Tribe Edition, 1982
Fourth Bear Tribe Edition, 1984
Fifth Bear Tribe Edition, 1986
Sixth Bear Tribe Edition, 1988
Seventh Bear Tribe Edition, 1989
Eighth Bear Tribe Edition, 1991

Published by Bear Tribe Publishing Company,
P.O. Box 9167, Spokane, Washington 99209

TABLE OF CONTENTS

ILLUSTRATIONS

INTRODUCTION

This book is not written by an anthropologist, but by an American Indian. It is not about one tribe, but a composite of many. It is knowledge I have learned from and about my people. It belongs to them, and credits are to the American Indians.

The name of this book is **BUFFALO HEARTS**. To many American Indians, the Buffalo was the center of his existence. He provided the Indian with everything -- meat for food, bones to make utensils, and hides for clothes and tents. The strength of the Buffalo symbolized the strength of the Indians. The Heart is the center of life.

I believe the American Indian was the freest, bravest man that ever lived. The Spanish spoke of the Indian as the bronze race that knew how to die.

The Indians refused to reproduce in slavery. That's why many California tribes perished, as well as all the Cuban Indians. A Spaniard once asked an Indian if he wanted to go to Heaven. The Indian replied, *"No because that's where the Spaniards go."*

To my people, freedom is not a political word that is bantered back and forth between Eastern and Western blocks of nations. Freedom is sitting on a horse on a hilltop and smelling the fresh wind in his face. Freedom is looking across a hundred miles of wilderness expanse. Freedom is something that no man can take from you or give to you.

When a certain band was about to be traded out of land and given a reservation, their chief's reply was, *"Is, the white man my creator, that he should set boundaries and tell me where I should go? No, the Great Spirit gave me this land and here I shall stay."*

The Shoshone chief Washakie was called in to talk treaty and was offered a reservation. His reply was, *"The Great Spirit made me an Indian, but not a reservation Indian. . . . . !"* With that he drove a knife into the treaty paper and walked out.

The Indian sense of land value and concept of land was entirely different from that of the invaders who came from across the Big Water. In speaking of the Earth, he said, *"The Earth is your Mother. You do not sell your Mother."*

The Indian regarded himself as a keeper and caretaker of the land for future generations. How different from a people who have so rushed to make a profit and pile up ulcers, that they have now polluted and wasted the land and do not know whether there are enough of our natural resources to last to the year 2000, just thirty short years from now.

Yet valuable resources are being wasted in foolish wars. The air is being polluted, water resources contaminated beyond use. Noise has become a health hazard in many areas.

And what of the American Indian? He was an extreme conservationist. He rarely killed anything he didn't eat. He offered a prayer before going to the hunt. *"We have to take your life in order to continue our own, Little Brother,"* he said to the deer. The Buffalo Dance was held in honor of the buffalo, and named the Buffalo Calling. A Deer Dance was held to invite and honor the deer.

In harvesting herbs and plants, the Indian would never take from the first plant he saw, but, offering a prayer, he would go on to the next, thus insuring the survival of the species.

There are Indian legends telling what happened to people who were bad and wasteful, and to the greedy. Like one old chief said, *"How come the white man got the country for nothing and now he owes everyone for it?"*

I remember when I was in the fourth grade, there was a picture in my history book. It showed two Spaniards torturing an Indian. The caption under the picture read, *"Two Spaniards torturing a savage to find out where the gold was hidden."*

The only savages I know are the same who planted wheat year after year until they destroyed the productivity of the land. We called them wheat savages.

I remember in the fall of the year in Dakota, when the whole prairie would be on fire, and I'd ask my mother what it was that did it. She said, *"They are burning off the wheat stubble."*

Then the terrible droughts of the thirties came, and the prairie states blew away, and the topsoil was gone.

When the first Europeans came to this country, the Indians treated them royally. Their philosophy was to treat the stranger as the Great Spirit in disguise. The early arrivals got puffed up and said, *"Oh these primitive savages think we're gods."*

The settlers sat down to make treaties with the Indians. They said, *"We want to use and share your land with you. We want to be brothers."*

The Indian brought and exchanged gifts, but later these white men were not satisfied with what land they had, and they said, *"We want more of your land."* And they started to misuse the Indians. The Indians said, *"We want our gifts back. You've broken our agreement and made a lie of our solemn gifts."* I believe that here was where the expression "Indian-giver" originated.

When the pilgrims first arrived, Squanto, a Sachem. befriended them. He tried to teach them agricultural Indian ways. He would put waste fish parts and whole fish in each hill of corn. He said, *"You have to feed the ground."* He meant that you can't just take and take. You have to give back to the earth if you want to continue to reap from it.

The pilgrims looked at Squanto's effort and said, *"Oh this is just some savage superstition. This is rich virgin soil."* It wasn't until the New England states had eroded away that they knew what Squanto was talking about.

Here was a conflict of cultures. The Indian was a man of stone -- unchanging -- believing that honesty and principal were unchangeable. The white man was a man of metal, malleable and changeable. His motto was that the end justified the means. He spoke with a forked tongue -- out of the side of his mouth. To the Indians he spoke of being brothers. To his fellow colonists he said, *"These are primitive, heathen savages to be exploited, lied to and slain."*

So when the man of stone came up against the man of metal, he was destroyed, and this pattern continued. However, not without resistance, for the Indian loved his family and his Earth Mother. And so, ill-armed and out-numbered, he fought with skill, cunning and courage.

It cost the United States 8 federal soldiers for every Indian killed. The Seminole Indian War cost this country $40 million, and only about 40 Seminoles were killed. Soldiers died like flies in the malarial swamps, and they lost millions of dollars worth of equipment.

Then the Army tried trickery to trap Osceola, bringing him in under a flag of truce, making him prisoner, and then beating him until he died, trying to force him to surrender his people. He refused, and the Seminoles are still in Florida today.

What is an American Indian? Today you see some people in the Big City of New York who are fair-skinned, and yet they retain their Indian language and culture. They dress and look like anyone else. They speak with a Brooklyn accent. Yet they are Mohawks, after 400 years of non-Indian domination.

Indians still retain their culture, and they are still Indians. There is a renaissance going on among the Indians. Today, Indians in New York have dance and pow wow groups. In Los Angeles, there are five major Indian dance groups that put on pow wows every weekend. You can go to an Indian pow wow in San Francisco, Chicago, Oakland, Seattle, or Denver, and many more places.

In the reservation areas as well, young people are asking their elders to teach them their ways. They say there were more tipis this year at the Sun Dance and the Crow Fair, and Indians are becoming proud again. There was less drinking at Gallup this year at the Ceremonial.

You see Indians driving heavy equipment and working in many kinds of jobs. Yet many carry their medicine around their necks, or wear Indian jewelry to show that they are Indian.

Today, we are 600,000 people, out of what was once 2 million who were slaughtered by deceit. In 1900, this was reduced to only 300,000. Up until 1900, many white men said *"The only good Indian is a dead Indian."*

So now we sit upon reservations -- 55 million acres of what was once our whole land. But today, there is a return of the spirit, a new generation and a new way -- but based on an ancient belief. And the white man is coming to see that, in some ways, if he is to survive, he must learn from the Indian.

He must learn to take better care of the land. He must reverse all of his greedy practices and learn a responsibility to the Earth mother. And he must learn that the earth is truly his mother and that he must share it with winged ones, and the four-leggeds, and with the fish as well. That hawks and coyotes and cougars are not to be killed needlessly. That there is beauty and value in a desolate place left just as it is.

Let his greed and arrogance disappear and let him say, *"The Earth is our Mother."* Then man will come alive again.

Chapter 1

SOME INDIAN LEGENDS

The Indian legends or stories are varied from tribe to tribe, but many have rich meanings.

Around Pyramid Lake (Nevada) the Paiutes tell of the Water Babies. In walking around the lake or on the bank of the Truckee River you can see their tracks -- small tracks, like a baby's. One time a man set a trap to catch an animal and instead caught a Water Baby. The next morning there was blood near the trap and the steel trap was broken in little pieces. Water Baby had broken the trap and escaped.

My friend Willie Astor, a Washoe Indian, told me several legends of his tribe. One is about how the Washoes got pine nuts.

There was a time when all the pine nut trees were only in one area and this was guarded by two old women. They were very selfish and wouldn't let the Indians have the pine nuts for food. The animals and birds felt sorry for the Indians and held a council, and each tried to find a way to help them. Then Raven decided he could help. He had a very bad sore under his wing and in this, he placed pine nuts. The old women looked at the sore when he passed out of the area and said, *"Ugh, it's ugly!"* and they let him pass. When he got out, he planted the pine nuts in the ground so the Washoes now have pine nuts to eat.

WHY THE BOBCAT'S FACE IS FLAT

One time when Bobcat was fast asleep under a tree, Coyote came along. Now Coyote is a very wise one, but he is also a trickster. So he decided to play a joke on Bobcat. First he sang a magic song so

Bobcat would sleep very deep. Then he started pushing on his face and the more he pushed, the flatter it got.

When Bobcat woke up, he felt funny and smelled Coyote all around. He said, *"Oh-oh, that trickster has been up to something."* Then he went to a stream and looked at his reflection. *"Waugh! That Coyote has made my face flat."* He said, *'I'll fix him for this."*

So he waited until he found Coyote asleep. Bobcat sang his magic song. Then he pulled on Coyote's nose and it got longer and longer. That's why the Bobcat's face is flat and Coyote's nose is long.

WHY THE WASHOE HAVE FIVE FINGERS ON THEIR HANDS

Once in the world there were only animals. The animals held a council and decided to make people. As they went along making people, everything was fine until they came to make the hands. Then an argument came up between Lizard and Coyote. The Coyote said, *"Let's make their front feet like mine. See? They are so good. I can dig with them or run fast."* Lizard said, *"No, make them like mine. I can grab things and hold very fast."*

Coyote got angry and chased Lizard into the rocks. Lizard crawled between the rocks and Coyote built a fire to force Lizard out. Just when the fire was hottest, Lizard climbed high above the fire and he waved to the animals and said, *"Here I am."* The animals saw Lizard's waving hands and they all said, *"Lizard wins."* That is why the Washoe have hands like the Lizard with five fingers.

It is the custom of my people, when sitting around the fire and telling stories at night that, when one has finished, another person would say, *"I'll tie another on to that."*

First I will tell you of our storyteller. The storytellers were much loved and respected among all tribes. Among my people he is called Yenadizee or Storm Fool. Sometimes a good storyteller would travel from camp to camp telling stories. He was always welcome and there was always a pot of stew for him.

From my people, the Chippewa, came these stories:

HOW THE BEAR CLAN BECAME THE MEDICINE CLAN

Once an old man came to the tribe and he was very sick and had sores all over his body. Because they looked so bad, no one would take him in and care for him. Each place he stopped and each clan he visited, they would turn him away. *"Oh you look so terrible. Go away, old man. We might catch a horrible sickness from you."*

Finally he sat down outside a village where a wigwam sat off by itself. An older woman of the Bear clan lived there by herself. She came out of her lodge and saw him. She said, *"Oh, Grandfather, you look very sick and tired. Come in and I will feed you and give you a place to sleep."* She took care of him and fed him and he slept there that night.

In the morning he told her to go into the forest and gather herbs for poultices to make his sores well, and they healed up. Then he got sick with another sickness and he sent her out after teas to make him well. And thus he did until he had had all the sicknesses known to mankind at that time.

Then he told her that he was a spirit person, and that he had come to teach the tribe medicine, and that ever after this, the Bear clan should be the medicine clan and know how to heal.

HOW THE PEACE PIPE CAME TO THE TRIBES (CHIPPEWA)

Once in the long time past, the tribes had been at war with each other for many years. When they met on the battlefield, many were slain on both sides. The Great Spirit looked down and was angry at their foolish wars.

Then the Great Spirit said, *"Look, the ground is red with blood. You must stop your battles. I will turn this ground to stone, and from this red stone you will make peace pipes.*

Whenever you have war or hatred in your hearts, you will smoke these and peace will come among you again."

There is another story of the peace pipe. I will tell it here.

Two tribes had been at war for a long time, and neither side wanted to be the first to make peace. But the peace chiefs had called them to council.

The warriors and war chiefs gathered in a circle. When the pipe

was passed around the circle, neither tribe would take it. Then, on
the fourth time around a woman with a small child was walking by.
The child reached out and touched the pipe. Immediately the warriors accepted it, each one taking it and smoking it in turn.

HOSPITALITY

Once there lived a very brave and good young hunter. He and his
wife had their lodge off on a hilltop with the deep forest around them.
While he was away hunting, two women came into his lodge. They
sat by the fire, for the first snow had fallen and it was very cold.
His wife, being a proper wife, offered them hospitality such as there
was, for there was no food in the house. She said, *"Good Mothers,
here is hot tea."* They took it and drank all that she gave them without saying a word.

When her husband returned, he brought home some rabbits and
these were cooked. His guests were offered the stew pot and they
devoured everything, leaving nothing for their hosts whatever, so
that the man and his wife had only tea to drink. All winter long, the
women stayed, eating most of the food.

In the spring the hunter and his wife were very thin and hungry,
yet through the whole long winter, they had fed their guests without
a complaint. In the spring, the women told the couple that they
were spirit people come to test their hospitality and kindness. Because they had found them to be good and kind, the man would have
great wisdom to help others. Then they said they would send them
knowledge of new foods and gifts.

Chapter 2

INDIAN MEDICINE

To the Indian, medicine was many things. First, it was the knowledge of healing. The average medicine man had a knowledge of as many as 150 herbs, some of them powerful poisons, but used in small amounts, they served as medicine.

In a jar of Vicks, you'll find that everything but the petroleum jelly came from the old medicine bag. Quinine and codeine came from South American Indians.

Many herbs were used in teas. Catnip and red clover were used to relax a person to sleep. Peppermint was used to settle upset stomachs. Slippery Elm bark was given to pregnant women. And from our animal brothers we learned how certain kinds of mud and clay served as poultices to draw the poisons from infected areas. Sometimes herbs were crushed and used in poultices.

Manzanita berries were crushed and a tea was made from them and used on skin affected by poison oak, causing the rash to dry up.

Squaw tea, which grows wild on the sage brush areas in Nevada, Utah, and California, is used as a blood purifier. When a person was sick or had aches and pains, some tribes would dig a long trench in sand. A fire was built to heat the sand, and after the fire was removed, the person was put in the trench and covered with blankets and more hot sand.

THE SWEAT LODGE

The sweat lodge was a round house made of bent-over willows and brush. Sometimes birch bark was added. In more recent times, canvas covered the lodge. The entrance faced the East and had a cover flap. There was a hole dug inside.

When the sweat ceremony took place in the Great Plains and Rocky Mountain areas, this hole had sage or sweet grass in it. A fire was built outside and large rocks were put in the fire to heat. River rocks were preferred because they wouldn't break as easily from the heat. When the rocks were hot, they were pushed out of the fire and into the lodge fire-hole with a green forked stick. When the rocks rolled onto the sweet grass and sage, it would fill the air with fragrance. At this time the patient and other participants breathed in the good smell.

When one person is to be treated alone, he goes in by himself, sometimes accompanied by a medicine man. In some tribes, the men use the sweat lodge to cleanse themselves on a daily or weekly basis and they smoke and sing together inside.

In entering the lodge, everyone enters clockwise, and they leave in a counter-clockwise direction. Water is kept in a pottery or stone bowl. The water is thrown on the hot rocks to cause steam, or to cause the rocks to breathe, as some tribes say. Everyone rubbed his body with sage or sweet grass and is given all the water he can drink. This way the men are cleansed from the inside out, and they have all fasted for at least one day. (On the west coast heat was used in the sweat house, but steam was rarely made with water and hot rocks).

In ceremonial use of the sweat, the participants fasted for four days prior to the sweat bath. Prayers were offered at that time for the sick.

The sweating is used for sinus and other breathing problems, and for lumbago, aches and pains. Old bones feel new again.

The fourth time the flap is opened, everyone files out. There is either a nearby river pond, or if the lodge is a back yard, there is a garden hose. Everyone washes off with cold water and dries off. If the sweat was ceremonial, a meal followed.

A group of Sioux men in a sweat lodge with the covering partly raised, showing the willow framework. 1898. Courtesy *Bureau of American Ethnology.*

Wooden sweat lodge frame and sacrificial pole used in connection with Ghost Dance. Pine Ridge, S.D. 1892. Courtesy *Bureau of American Ethnology.*

PEYOTE MEDICINE

The peyote cactus is used for medicine. The buttons are eaten green or dry, or ground up in a mash, or boiled in a tea. The peyote is very bitter.

A dry button has a cotton in it. Some people take this out and throw it away, but many peyote people eat the whole button.

Peyote tea is good for colds, flu, and other sickness.

But peyote is used more as a sacrament and medicine by the Native North American Church.

In peyote meetings, group prayer and healing is done. Sometimes several people who are sick are brought to the same meeting which is held in a house, tipi, or hogan.

The last meeting I attended used the Cheyenne half moon altar. The Father Peyote was placed on the half moon. The meeting was held in a tipi behind some brush at an Indian family's home, not 200 yards from a busy highway.

The meeting didn't start until about ten o'clock in the evening. This meeting had been requested by a lady, to have us pray for her sickness. Other sick people also came. But the lady provided the food and peyote.

We sat on the ground in the tipi. The youngest of us was an eight year old boy, and the ages went on up from there.

The peyote drum is a water kettle drum. An iron kettle full of water had a wet piece of hide stretched over it. More water is sucked by mouth up into the drum head from time to time. The wetness gives it a special tone. Anyone familiar with drums will recognize the peyote drum beat immediately when they hear it.

A fire was kept burning near the altar. After everyone was seated in the tipi, the peyote was brought in. They were large green buttons. A basket full of buttons was passed around, and everyone took some.

The people who were used to using peyote bit into it and ate it like apples. But those of us not used to it ate much more slowly.

Then the peyote priest told us why the meeting was. *"We have come here to pray and help this woman who is sick. But we will say prayers for everyone."* The drum was ready. The man next to the drummer took his peyote fan in his hand. It was made of flicker tail feathers. He also had a round gourd rattle tasseled with horse hair and beaded around the handle. He sang four songs, and then the drum was passed to the next pair of singers, along with the other paraphernalia, and they sang their four songs. The drum, fan and rattle were passed this way until everyone had sung their songs.

When the drum was passed to a man who had no one to drum for his songs, he asked someone to come over to drum for him.

Every singer has his own fan and rattle.

The peyote priest spoke again. He said, *"I'm going to make a smoke for this lady."* And while he spoke, he rolled a cigarette of tobacco with a little cedar or sage mixed in it. He used corn husks for rolling this ceremonial smoke. He continued, *"This lady has been sick a long time. She is a good woman and she wants to be well so she can enjoy her life and take care of her family.* The lady said, *"Yes that's what I want."* She was crying some.

Then the leader said, *"Now I'm going to offer a prayer in my language. First I will tell you in English so you will know."* He was smoking and offering the smoke all the time he was praying. *"Now, God and Jesus please listen and hear this prayer."* Then he began praying in the Ute language. He said, *"Shunkah, bless her."* He prayed for twenty minutes or so.

Another person said he would like to offer a prayer for the woman. Then someone else said, *"I would like to offer a prayer in my language for all the people here."* So he prayed in Washoe and he indicated each person. He said, *"I'm going to pray for this man and his wife. I do not know them but they've come a long way and we're all glad to have them here and want them to come again. I pray for my friend Joe. He is a good man and takes good care of his family. Bless him. I pray for my son in Vietnam. And for my sister's boy in jail. May things go well for him."* This is the way they prayed, with great humility.

In the night more peyote was passed around. Peyote tea was served. More prayers were offered and the songs were sung again.

Sometimes when first taking peyote, called medicine by the Indian people, a man goes outside and vomits, or digs a hole in front of himself to cough up the poison that the medicine draws out of his body.

The chanting and singing, the giving of smokes and praying goes on until morning. At dawn the meeting ended and the people went outside for stretching and visiting. They stayed around for the peyote feast. At noon a big meal was served.

In some peyote meetings, there is a ceremonial breakfast. First, water is passed. Each person takes some and drinks, and he takes corn, meat, and fruit, as each is passed. The peyote priest tells how these are gifts from the Great Spirit so that everyone will live well.

Sometimes gifts are brought to the peyote priest.

OTHER CEREMONIES AND HEALING

In the ceremony of the Eastern tribes, there is a staff of life. A literal wood staff is passed around and this is held by the singers as they sing. It must make a complete circle as it travels the circle of life. It may make as many as three or four circles in a night.

The peyote religion is legal in all States for the Indian people. Some people have tried to make it illegal. But we contend that if wine is a legal sacrament to churches, then peyote is proper for the Indians. It is not a narcotic or a drug. Spiritual users of peyote do not drink alcohol.

There are many other tribes that have a shaman or medicine men. Some tribes, like the Pomo in Northern California, have medicine women. The Navajo use many herbs and they also make prayers with sandpainting. They have their nine-day healing ceremony and the night chants.

The Pomo, among others, suck the poison and sickness out of the bodies of the afflicted.

Much of our medicine knowledge is gone or lost. The knowledge to heal a badly wounded man was used by the Pawnee and other Plains tribes. They would shoot a man to prove their power. People would see blood pouring from the wound and the wounded man would be dying, and yet the medicine man would make him completely alive.

A man in the Crow tribe, who had no hair on his head, prayed, and in a vision was told to wear a buffalo cap. When he took the cap off after he wore it for a year, his hair was long enough to reach out and around his tipi.

Strange thing? No, when these men lived, they were not bombarded by noise or television or car horns honking. And so they were much closer to nature and with the Great Unseen. They were able to call on powers that today are unknown and not believed in.

Chapter 3

BELIEFS

The rules of the Indian society were to give a man strength, to make him a better person. He had rules of fasting to develop him spiritually, and his greatest punishment was disapproval by the tribe, or to be ostracized.

The rules of this American society exist because of its weaknesses. You need a policeman on the street corner to protect you from the man across the street.

The Indians' laws regarding his relationship with his fellow tribesmen were recorded in his heart. They were not written on tablets of stone or in law books. Each man carried the law in his heart. This is truly the only good law.

This lawless society has a lot to learn from the American Indian. The Indian took pride in himself as an individual, in his abilities and skills.

The young man was taught to be proud of his work and his honor. When he did an outstanding achievement, the tribe would proclaim it. *"This young man has returned from his first hunt and has killed his first buffalo."* Maybe at an earlier age, his parents would take pride in his bringing home his first rabbit. He was showing ability in important life skills.

When he was 14, he would go out alone to fast for four days and nights. He would ask for a vision. He would pray, *"I am poor and alone without garments. I seek a vision. Who will be my guide, my keepers?"*

If his heart was good, maybe some animal will come and answer

Three masks of the Iroquois False Face Society. The first mask on
the left belonged to the Mohawk leader Joseph Brant. The center
mask is an Onondaga Harvest Mask. The example on the right is a
Seneca Scalp Mask.

Courtesy *Museum of the American Indian.*

him in a vision. Or maybe a spirit will come and give him a vision or the thunder would talk to him. Then he could return to the village.

The medicine man would put him in the sweat lodge, and then announce his new name, according to the vision, or, as in some cases, he would have a secret name known only to him. Then when he got older and did something outstanding, his childhood name of Little Rabbit might be changed to Brave Bull.

The young women at the time when they came to puberty were regarded with new respect. For here were the mothers of future warriors. Their learning of household skills was past the play stage. They were taught all they needed to know in life – preparation of food, making tipis and clothing, and above all, industry. A lazy woman was held in contempt. At the time when girls were 15 or 16 years old, young men would start courting, and old Dad would look them over. The young man might bring horses, or he might drop a deer for a gift for his future father-in-law, this way showing that he would be a good provider. There was no welfare for the couple to go to after they were married. And no one wanted a bum for a son-in-law. So they looked very carefully at this new prospective son-in-law.

To the Indian people, sex was a perfectly natural thing in the relationship between two people. It was something that their Little Brothers, the animals did to reproduce, and they did it too. It wasn't something of the double standard or the holier than thou attitude held by some people. And it wasn't dirty pictures on outhouse walls. There were no frustrated, mixed-up people. Yet in some tribes purity was taught so that sex would not be used just for pleasure, and children would have the protection of both father and mother.

Sex is symbolized by the Navajo when they refer to the light and heavy rains as the He and She rains. The Squash Blossom necklaces worn by Navajo men and women represent fertility.

In the Southwest, the Green Corn Ceremony is held when the new corn is ready for eating. This is the time when marriages were witnessed by the whole tribe. The couple may have been living together for some time in trial marriage. But now they announced to the tribe that they intended to make a lasting thing of it.

With my tribe, the Chippewa, the women would remove their clothing and circle the corn fields at night to give it a blessing for fertility and protection. In the Southwest, the old way was to watch the sun-watcher peaks. Then when the sun had reached its furthest south point, all the fires were put to sleep and restarted in the old way. This is the time for many celebrations and ceremonies -- the time of the Return of the sun. It is a time of rejoicing, for now comes the blending or remating of Father Sun and the Earth Mother. If the sun did not return, there would be no growth of new life. It's this union of Earth and Sun that means life.

The American Indian had a very close relationship with the land. He believed in blending with nature rather than trying to conquer it. He felt that he shared the land with his fellows and the animals and winged life around him.

Once when out acting as a hunting guide, an Indian had lost his direction home. The white man with him said, *"You're lost, Chief."* The Indian replied, *"Indian not lost. Tipi lost."* And that was true wherever the night found him. He was at home and would lie down and sleep.

Five-sevenths of the vegetables of the world were developed by the American Indian. In planting a garden, the Indians believed in disturbing the top soil as little as possible. Back in timber country you see Indian gardens planted between the stumps. Holes were chopped here and there for the seeds. They were really good gardens.

The Hopi Indians live in northern Arizona. Their country is a great, dry expanse. But the Hopi have been agricultural for centuries.

Back in the 1930's, the federal government decided it was going to teach the Hopi how to raise corn. So they came out with tractors and tore up the ground, planted Iowa hybrid corn. The corn grew up tall. Then the hot northern Arizona winds blew, and that was the end of the government corn. The Hopi had planted their corn the same way as always, and they had corn. As one of my friends says, the Hopi plant their corn on a rock with a prayer and it grows. And that's the way it seems.

The Hopi plant their corn maybe a foot deep in the ground. Their fields are little catch basins with dams along the lower end, for catching what winter moisture there is. As the corn grows, the Hopi hill it up to protect it from the strong winds.

Their corn is many colors. They have white, yellow, red, blue, black, and then they combine all the colors on one ear. They know how to grow corn, and they cook it green or dry. They grind it and make meal and flour. They make their thin flat Pike bread which they serve rolled up.

The Hopi are called *"the Peaceful Ones."* They have never engaged in war. They have avoided contact with the federal government as much as possible.

Back in the twenties and thirties, Hopi leaders were put in prisons for refusing to let their children attend Bureau of Indian Affairs schools. The Hopi felt that taking their young ones away during their formative years would ruin them. Of course, it's possible they were right.

The traditional people are very strong among the Hopi, and it's this that has kept the tribe together.

Hopi Snake Dances are performed each year. This is a very sacred dance. The Hopi priests gather up the snakes, the rattlesnake being used most often. The snakes are placed in a pit with a cover over it. And then, as the Hopi pass over it, they stomp on it to let the snakes know they are invited to the dance.

After a while, the Hopi take up the snakes and place them in their mouths. One holds the snake in his mouth while another dancer comes along beside him and strokes him with a feather to let him know all is well. After dancing with the snakes, the Hopi run out carrying the snakes in their mouths, and release them in the desert. The snakes then act as messengers to the gods, letting them know of the Hopi prayers for rain.

The Hopi make the Kachina dolls. These represent the Mountain People or spirits. There are Kachinas for everything. Then when the Hopi hold the Kachina ceremonies, the priests dress like the Kachina and they give the dolls as gifts to the children from behind the masks. This is to teach the children to be kind and generous and give things to one another.

The Iroquois of New York State used to carve masks on a living tree. Then when they removed the mask, the spirit of the tree would remain in the mask. These were the masks of the False Face Society. They were carved in very grotesque shapes. From behind these masks, the Iroquois would work to cure their sick. They also had corn husk masks which are used similarly.

The Iroquois had beautiful gardens and many fine orchards. When the Europeans first came to this country, they were able to give the new settlers the knowledge of raising crops.

The Chippewa had three different degrees of medicine men -- the Joskeed, Wabeno, and Medas. Some work with plants and herbs, and some with medicine chants and sweat baths. But even teaching is medicine, we say. Knowledge is healing. If you help someone to a better knowledge so they can make a better life and living, then you are healing them.

The Chippewa had what they called the Ojeebe rites. In this a medicine man would go into his lodge and chant and pray. He would ask for his spirit helper to give him the help he needed. And pretty soon you would hear voices, and sometimes the lodge would vibrate and rise up off the ground. When the medicine man came out, he would use the knowledge that the spirit gave him, to heal the patient, or to help him to do what was needed.

Lots of times when people got lost, the old medicine men would be consulted. Even the forest rangers would come out and ask him where to find the lost person. And he would go in and chant, and then come out. *"The man you are looking for is lying over there near the north end of the lake,"* or *"He is dead and you will find his body such and such a place."* And there it would be.

They used this same knowledge to find game in the winter when it was scarce. The medicine man would say, *"Go over to the north end of the swamp, and you will find a big deer standing there. Shoot him and we will have meat in the camp."*

The Sioux medicine man was consulted in regard to the buffalo hunt. He would fast and offer prayers to locate the buffalo. With most other tribes the medicine man was always consulted in regard to the hunt. And each hunter had his own medicine that he carried for success in the hunt.

Chapter 4

MY PEOPLE AND THINGS ABOUT THEM

The American Indian took pride in his body. He had a body with nice, smooth, even muscles. He wasn't muscle-bound or over-developed like some weight lifters. His muscles were used in every day activity. He used all his muscles in hunting, running, swimming, ball playing, and all Indian sports.

I remember my father and uncles used to swim a mile across a lake and back with only a brief rest in between. They worked in the woods, logging and cutting timber, and pulling a saw back and forth all day, which gave them good arm and stomach muscles.

Jim Thorpe, the All-Around Olympic Champion, brought much honor to his Indian people. This is remarkable when you realize that he was the outstanding athlete of the 300,000 people competing against him.

Indian runners have been showing their endurance and ability for hundreds of years. Indian runners were used between forts in the early days of the "Old West" and it wasn't thought unusual for them to run 125 miles in one run, without resting. In the 1930's, a Chippewa runner ran 225 miles the same way.

Among the Hopi, men in their 60's and 70's run 45 and 50 miles a day to work their fields.

The Indian, in hunting, often covered 40 or 50 miles in a day. He hunted until he found food. Sometimes he would be out for days, in all kinds of weather.

In the winter, the Indian hunter would try to find shelter behind fallen trees, or a cave and build himself a small fire to keep as warm as possible. But at times, out on the prairie, he would curl up under his robe, sometimes sleeping under snow drifts or whatever, to keep warm. Survival was a tough business.

The Indians tried to prepare for the winter as well as possible. If the fall and summer hunts had been good, there was plenty of jerky, dried berries, and corn, squash, or beans -- depending upon which tribe it might be.

When the hunters returned home to the camp, things were always better. If the hunt was a success, there was fresh meat and stories to tell to the other people of the hunt. *"I saw a lot of elk or deer up near the north mountain slope,"* one might say. Or, *"No game, but tomorrow will be another day. Tonight I will offer new prayers."*

The Indian was expert as a still hunter. He would conceal himself by a water hole and wait all day long, with a bow and arrow or a lance. He had to be close to his game, and there was no second chance. He either made a kill, or the deer was up and running away. This type of hunting took a lot of skill and patience.

Another method was stalking. In stalking, after spotting the game, we always come in against the wind so the game could not smell us. But sometimes cover was the most important thing, because by rubbing ourselves with sage and having a bath, there isn't so much man smell. We always keep brush or rocks between ourselves and the game and try to move only when they are grazing or looking away. We belly crawl or bend down low for close range stalking, and put brush in our hair or hat bands. When we put brush all around our bodies, it breaks up our outline and makes for better stalking.

In warfare the Indian was able to conceal himself even out on the seemingly bare prairie.

For fishing, the Indian made fish hooks out of hard wood, rock, or bone. His lines were tough sinew or fiber cord. He used nets in many places, and Indian-type fish traps are still in use today. Many Indian people speared and gaff-hooked fish during the spawning season.

Some tribes fished through the ice in winter. His fish was grilled or baked when fresh-caught. Some tribes would wrap the fish in clay or mud and bake it. Some dug pits and wrapped the fish in leaves and placed them over beds of coals to roast, covering everything with sand. This was a way to roast camas bulbs, corn, and potatoes as well.

If it was the time of a big salmon run, the whole tribe would get together, and there would be feasting and games to play. Gambling was always part of their enjoyment, as well as sports and canoe races.

The salmon was king with the Northwest Coast tribes who lived good lives. Of course they ate other fish and clams, wild fruits, deer and other game, acorn soup and biscuits. There were Potlatch feasts where families would give away great wealth, in this way showing how generous they were. The government stopped this among the Canadian Indians, but there has been some revival of this custom in the last few years.

The Northwest Coast Indians used long cedar canoes carved out of cedar logs, with the outside beautifully ornamented, carved, and painted. These people also carved totem poles which were used as front panels on their houses. These poles told the history of the clan. They carved utensils out of wood, such as the Potlatch bowls and spoons. The totem represented the family clan. Among most northwest tribes, the clan system was in effect. An Indian could not marry anyone from his own clan or his mother's clan. This prevented inter-breeding. With many tribes, inheritance is passed through the mother.

Among the Navajo, when a man marries, he moves to his wife's family, and it is the wife who owns the sheep. The wealth stays with her family. The children belong with her, and her brothers correct them and teach them as well.

In my tribe there are many clans: the Bear clan which is the medicine clan, the Crane clan, Manfish clan, Otter, Heron, and others. In some tribes, the clan system is still kept up, and you will hear people refer to someone as his clan sister or clan brother. The clan and the family are very tight social structures and there is a very deep love of family with Indian people. There is no such thing as an unwanted child, and children born out of wedlock do not have a social stigma attached to them. They are accepted and loved by the family, the clan, and the tribe.

Indians are great child psychologists. They spend time with their children loving them and they don't give their children the back of the hand. They don't say, *"Don't bother me,"* when the child wants to ask a question. They take the time to explain things. When a child is asking, is the time to answer. Even today, the Indians don't

leave their children home with a babysitter when a pow wow comes
up. The whole family goes, and you see little kids 4 or 5 years old
out there dancing. They are part of it all and they learn from the older people.

Many tribes make beautiful beadwork. I know how much effort
my cousin spent on his son's outfit, and now they proudly dance together.

The sense of responsibility to one another was an important thing.
When a man returned from the hunt, he shared with the rest of the
people. The spirit of sharing was strong among us. I do not think
that the measure of a civilization is how tall its buildings of concrete
are, but rather on how well its people have learned to relate to their
environment and fellow man. In this, the American Indians were far
superior to this present society.

GOVERNMENT

At the time when Europeans were still serving as serfs and vassels,
American Indians had a democracy that was functioning. The Iroquois
Six Nation Confederacy was set up to abolish war between all tribes.
It started out as a Five Nation Confederacy. It was established about
1390, one hundred years before the arrival of Columbus. In the Confederacy it was the clan mothers who selected the chiefs. Each nation
or tribe could select nine chiefs and one war chief. The women could
also depose or recall these chiefs for improper behavior.

In their Confederacy, there was a women's council. If the women
felt that their family representative wasn't acting in their best interest,
they told the war chief, and he informed the chief. Then if he didn't
straighten up, they asked that he be removed. The Confederacy was
set up to establish the Great Peace and other tribes came in volun-
tarily. The Iroquois extended to them the benefits and blessings of
the Confederacy, but only the original member tribes had a voice in
the Confederacy.

The Confederacy was divided into two sections, two tribes to each.
The fifth tribe was known as the fire keepers tribe. This was the
Onondaga. If both sections of the Confederacy agreed on a decision,
it was then referred to the fire keepers. If they found anything they
disagreed with, it was referred back to the four tribe council. Then if

the chiefs of the council still agreed, the decision was passed, even if the fire keepers still disagreed.

When there was disagreement between the two sections, it was referred to the fire keepers to break the deadlock. This was so that in the end there must be an agreement.

If another tribe wished to join the Great Peace, they were accepted. They were allowed to keep their religion and festivals. But they had no voice in the government. This was to keep the Confederacy strong and from being corrupted by outside influences. If the Iroquois asked a tribe to cease from fighting and killing and accept the Great Peace, they were to have their warriors concealed. Then the war chief was to ask the chief of the enemy tribe three times to accept peace, and after asking the third time, if he refused, the war chief of the Iroquois could strike him and kill him. And this would be a declaration of war. The Confederacy was to continue to fight until the other tribe was beaten. Then all weapons would be taken from that tribe, and they would be taught the ways of peace.

The Iroquois laws are recorded on belts of wampum beads. The teaching of these was passed on orally to the new chiefs. While holding the belt, they would be reminded of what section of law this belt represented. The belt representing the Great Peace was of white wampum. Many of the others were blue and white or purple and white.

When Deganawida and Hiawatha went up against Adadarhoh, they relied on healing songs to heal him of his wicked ways, rather than slaying him by chopping his head off, as was the custom in England and other so-called civilized countries. Adadarhoh was a wicked sorcerer who ate human flesh and hated all the Indians and disrupted all their efforts toward peace. His body was all crooked as well. So Deganawida and Hiawatha sang songs and converted him to the idea of the Great Peace. They also healed his body and he became a great leader for the peace.

Among the Plains Indians, a man was chief only as long as he did the will of the people. If he got to be too chiefy, he'd go to sleep one night, and wake up the next morning to find that he was chief all to himself. The tribe would move away in the night, and they didn't wait four years to do it either.

Coiffures de danse des habitans de la Californie.

**Central California Indians with dance headdresses (early 1800's).
Courtesy** *Bancroft Library, Univ. of California.*

Chapter 5

WARRIORS AND WAR

The American Indian fought bravely for his lands. The chiefs did not plot the battles from a safe place behind the lines. They were in the forefront and the foremost in battle. They lead their warriors. And the warriors weren't drafted -- they all volunteered.

When a war chief got ready to go on the warpath, he would tell the reasons for this war party, and the braves would say, *"I'll go."* And if he was not a good leader, the braves might not follow him again. If they went out on the warpath and the chief lost too many men, it was not good. If he could lead a raid and bring back all his men safely, that was a very successful raid and more men would follow him.

When the British and French went to fight the Indians, they lined up in a long line. This was proper European fashion for fighting a war, with a drummer at the end of the line. But the Indians fought from behind whatever concealment was available. It was from the American Indian that this country learned guerrilla warfare. The American Indian knew what he was fighting for -- his way of life, for his land, his family, and his freedom.

The Plains Indian and his horse had a unique togetherness. When the Spanish brought horses north, it was the Comanches who first got them, and it was the horse that gave the Comanches domination of the southern plains. They hunted buffalo on horseback with lances. They would ride alongside a buffalo and drive a sharp lance home to kill the buffalo.

With the horse, the Comanche was free to move, hunt, and raid where he pleased. It was the horse that gave the Sioux prominence.

One general called the Sioux the greatest light cavalry in the world.

In hunting, the Sioux had their buffalo ponies. They were trained for that and used for that exclusively. In war, they used their war ponies. These beautiful Indian ponies had great stamina.

An Indian boy would be given a colt when he was 5 to 6 years old, and he and his pony would grow up together. So well trained was the horse that the two acted as one unit. The pony would come when he was called. The boy could drop the reins and control the horse entirely with his knees or other signals. Often you would see little boys crawling up a leg to get on their horses, or leading them to a rock to mount. And the patient horse would wait until his little rider was mounted.

The Nez Perce tribe developed a special breed of horse, the Appaloosa. These beautiful spotted horses were mountain bred. They had broad chests and were tremendous runners. In fact, the United States Army so hated and feared the speed of the Appaloosa, that they slaughtered 800 head of Chief Joseph's horses!

The Cheyenne tribe was the one who first started using a rope sling around their horses' bodies. This is now called the Cheyenne rope. An Indian rider could slip down on the side of his horse's body, with only a heel of one foot hooked on the horse's back. The weight of his body was held up by the rope. It would look to the enemy at the wagon like a riderless horse. Then, riding in close, he could shoot from under the horse's neck. Of course, this took great horsemanship. But the Indian had this and a well-trained body. He could come on the run, press his hands on his pony's rump, and vault onto his back from the rear.

The tribes took great pride in their horses and would bet great sums on them in races.

In battle, a Cheyenne warrior would say, *"Remember the young and helpless ones and fight hard. For it's a good day to die."* If the fighting was going badly, a young brave would drive a stake in the ground with a rope fastened to it, and say, *"I will not move. I will fight here until my brothers rally, and fight back over me."* When others would see this young man riding to battle with a rope harness around him, they would say, *"He is about to do a brave thing. He carries his life in his teeth."*

The Cheyenne was called the Chopped Finger tribe. By other

Indians, this, in sign language was indicated by a motion like that of chopping off fingers. This was the Cheyenne's way because the young men would chop off and offer a finger to the Great Spirit in sacrifice. They would say, *"We cannot offer anything else. Everything already belongs to you. So we offer of ourselves."*

Among the Plains Indians, there were different societies whose job it was to protect and police the tribe while on the move. They were the scouts. Outstanding among these societies were the Dog Soldiers of the Cheyenne. The Dog Soldiers were the crack troops of the Cheyenne. They were the first to hit Custer and they held him back while the others grouped and prepared for battle. When Custer hit the Dog Soldiers, he saw the women and old people escaping to safety. Custer called, *"Hurry! The Indians are escaping. If you don't hurry there won't be enough Indians left to kill."* Then he got his surprise.

Custer once boasted that with his 7th Cavalry he would ride through the whole Sioux nation. Well, Custer hit the Sioux at three o'clock in the afternoon. The Sioux had pushed him up on a side hill. Custer ordered his men to dismount and fight on foot. By four-thirty, the battle was over. Some of Custer's men were drunk. The Sioux found whiskey in their flasks. The soldiers must have thought it was going to be a fun trip -- just ride in and slaughter Indians in their tipis.

Custer wouldn't listen to his scouts who said, *"Too many Indians."* He had split his command. Major Reno was to attack from the opposite side -- a maneuver intended to surround the Indians. Reno came up against the Sioux and they were too much for him. He retreated to some rocks and trees on a hilltop for shelter. When reinforcements came up the next day, the officer said, *"Assemble your command."* Reno said, *"They're here, sir."* He had 60 men alive of his command. Many of these were wounded.

Later, the Army tried to courtmartial Reno for failing to go to Custer's aid against more than 2000 Sioux and Cheyenne.

In warfare and horse raiding, one could gain honors or coup according to his achievements. The touching of a live enemy was considered a braver deed than to kill someone. Being the one to touch the first dead enemy in a battle was a brave thing because this showed you were in the front of the fight.

Among the Plains Indians a man was allowed to wear eagle feathers according to his achievement, and after much done in life, he might have a whole war bonnet showing his courage. Plenty Coups of the Crow had a bonnet plus a double trailer that touched the ground. Such was his courage in battle. And when he went into council wearing this bonnet with trailers, men would honor him by letting him be the first to speak.

War paint was used by many tribes. Each man had special markings and sometimes he would paint a red hand on his horse -- a symbol that he was out to revenge the death of a friend or relative. Sometimes the man would paint his bare chest as well, maybe hand marks or dots. Perhaps in a vision he had received a message telling him how to paint. The Apache would use black and yellow. Other tribes used red, black, white, and even blue.

Scalping did not start with the Indians. It came from the British. They paid their Indian allies for killing their enemies, and in order to have proof that they had killed French or enemy Indians, they had to bring the scalps. For these they were paid in trade goods of guns or rum. Of course an enterprising brave having trouble finding French scalps might just deliver British or American colonists' scalps, and this did happen as one British officer complained.

Scalping was also practiced by the Mexicans against the Apache. In fact, 17 American trappers joined with Mexican officials in slaughtering Apaches. They invited the Apache down to a fiesta at Santa Rita del Cobre and after feeding and giving drink to the Apaches, they fired cannon and guns into their midst. Some 400 people were killed -- men, women and children. These scalp hunters sold the scalps to the government of Chihuahua state. It was treatment like that which put the Apache on the warpath.

Some Indians used torture. So did the Americans, the French, the British, and the Spanish. The Indians felt if they made it distasteful enough, the invaders would stay out of their territory.

With some eastern tribes it was considered an honor to be tortured to test their courage. With my tribe this was true. We would say, *"Do you think I am fearful of you? Test my courage."*

The Indian decorated his war shield with symbols to protect him in battle. This was made of tough buffalo bull hide and had special medicine on it. Also he wore his medicine pouch to protect him in the battle. The tomahawk or warclub could be a simple one with a rock laced to the handle. Some were hand carved of hardwood with

a round wood ball on the end. Later the French made trade tomahawk or war axes with steel or bronze blades.

The Chippewa trade tomahawk had a pipe bowl at the top with the
tomahawk blade on the bottom.

The Indians took captives. These were adopted into the tribe, or
by individuals. Many times, if an Indian man had lost a son, he would
take a young boy on a raid and raise him up as his own. White and
Mexican girls who were captured would be raised up and marry into
the tribe. Many of these refused to return to their former homes, and
those who did return often regretted that decision as the Indian life
was so much freer.

Washakie, the Shoshone who heartily objected to the reservation system. 1804-1900. Photo circa 1882?

Courtesy *Bureau of American Ethnology*

Chapter 6

OUR NATIVE AMERICAN HEROES

In writing this section on our heroes, it has been a hard decision as to which leaders to write short sketches on. All of these men were great leaders, and so were others, even before the time of recorded American history. Unfortunately many of our old story tellers or oral historians are no longer available for our learning. Our birchbark and buffalo records are destroyed.

One of these days I should like to undertake a television series based on the lives of these men. I think that it is important that all people know the qualities of greatness of Native Americans. It is needed by our young people to inspire them to like greatness. The most important work anyone can undertake is to labor for the benefit of his people. One must reach out beyond himself. This is the true growth of humanity.

These are the men of Indian history whom we remember as great. Remember this; no matter how much given to violence or warfare these men might have been, they were not the aggressors. They were fighting for their homelands. I have wanted to tell their story for a long time – not as white writers saw them, but as I saw them, and as their own people saw them. I feel that this is my right. I want to tell it as I feel toward them. I am a Native American.

Geronimo.   1834-1909.   Died at Fort Sill, Oklahoma Territory,
February 17, 1909.

*Smithsonian Institution National Anthropological Archives, Bureau
of American Ethnology Collection.*

GERONIMO

At times people have said to me, *"Geronimo was a renegade or a bad guy, wasn't he?"* No, Geronimo was a patriot, a man who fought hard for his people. There were 60 million people in this country when Geronimo was fighting. He didn't expect to defeat the United States, but only to secure desert lands for his people and a just treaty. He belonged to the Mimbreno band of Apache. He was a good hunter and tracker and knew how to survive in the desert. They said of the Apache that they were equal on foot to any man on horseback. The Apache knew every water hole around the country. They knew which would be dry certain times of year. The Apache would carry water using the small intestine of the horse as a container. In warfare he also survived successfully.

They said a cavalry man would ride a horse 40 miles and the horse would be done. The Apache could ride a horse 60 miles and if the horse died or broke a leg, he would then use the horse as food. The cavalry man would be hit by a bullet and he'd be out of the fight. His body was all liquid. The Apache flesh was tough and hard like the hawk's. He would take two or three bullets in battle and yet walk away to heal up by a medicine man to fight another day. If he received a death wound in the stomach that he knew he couldn't survive, he asked to be left to cover his people's retreat, and to take all the enemies he could with him.

Geronimo was a medicine man besides being a great war chief.

What drove Geronimo to become a man of hatred and vengence? At one time the Apaches were on a peaceful trading mission. They took their women and children and old people along. They had furs and hides to trade for things they wanted. They camped outside the village of Janos in Chihuahua State. Unknown to them, they had been followed by Indian-hater General Carasco, the military governor of Sonora State. It didn't matter to him that he had no jurisdiction in the State of Chihuahua where the Apache were camped. He ordered his soldiers to charge with swords and bayonets, as he didn't want to attract the men Apaches by gunfire. So they killed and scalped the defenseless women and children and took what they wanted as captives to sell into slavery. Geronimo found his wife and three children among the slain. Here they were deep in Mexican territory without arms. Geronimo's heart was dead within him. He sat silently in

council. There was nothing they could do then. The Apache returned to Arizona quietly. But from then on Geronimo became a human
tiger.

Geronimo trusted no one, Mexican or American. He killed and
fought across the whole Apache land. Between Mexico and the
United States the two nations had 12,000 troops in the field. But
Geronimo raided wherever he wished.

The military, famous for their statistical body counts had a tough
time justifying their time spent hunting the Apache. The Apache
would fight as long as they wanted to, then break off the engagement
and disappear. The military would say, *"We got one or two bodies.
But of course the Apache carry away their dead."*

Out of Tucson, there was a ring of war profiteers who, whenever
the Apache would show signs of wanting peace, would create incidents to renew the fighting. Thus, when Geronimo was coming in to
surrender, a whiskey peddler was sent into his camp to get the warriors drunk and spread rumors among them. General Crook, an
honest American General, said all the trouble was caused by *"Greed
and avarice on the part of the whites."* In other words, the almighty
dollar is at the bottom of nine-tenths of all our Indian troubles. And
that was true from the start. First the white man allowed the Apache
several reservations, then he started pushing them all into San Carlos
because he wanted the other land.

General Crook was the most successful in fighting the Apache, and
his success in capturing Geronimo was due to his using Apache scouts
recruited from bands already settled onto reservations. But sad to relate, after Geronimo was captured, those faithful Apache scouts who
had served the Army so well were herded onto the same train and
sent to Florida where many Apache died. This was by orders from
higher up.

Back in 1933, some of the descendents of these scouts were suing
the government for wages that were promised to the scouts but never
paid. Again, the white man spoke with a forked tongue.

Arizona didn't become a state until 1912. This partly was due to
the Indian unrest. After being kept in Florida for a number of years,
Geronimo and his band were sent to Fort Sill, Oklahoma where Geronimo lived until his death. He was always an industrious man.
Whenever an artist wanted to paint his picture or someone wanted to

write of him, he collected money from them. And even in his old age, he was a good shot. He once bet an artist that he could hit a quarter at a great distance, and hit it he did.

He always would ask if any of his friends needed money back at San Carlos, and he'd send it to them.

He went to the Worlds Fair in Omaha, Nebraska where he was a great attraction. He sold little bows and arrows and other things he made. A Pima Indian woman whom I knew met him there. When he found out that her group of Indians were from Arizona, he wanted to buy them lunch and fruit. He was so glad to see Indian people from Arizona.

He once showed his body to an artist and he had some fifty bullet scars on his body. Some of them were deep enough that you could put a pebble into them. He believed in his medicine. He said, *"Bullets can't kill me."*

Geronimo lived in a time when this country believed that the only good Indian was a dead Indian. And because Geronimo was fighting for the country and Apache way that he loved, he was a bad Indian. To me, he was a brave warrior and patriot of his people.

On the Mexican Border, 1886. Geronimo, mounted left. Natchez mounted with hat.
Courtesy *Arizona Pioneers Historical Society Library.*

Appaloosas were taken north from Chihuahua, probably by the Navajo, and finally reached the Nez Perce country in the Columbia basin some two hundred years ago. The Nez Perces were excellent stockmen and had herds of the spotted horses when the first white men visited their country.

One of the centers of the Appaloosa herds was the rolling hill country along the Palouse river in southeastern Washington. White settlers began calling the horses Palouses, which changed in time to Appaloosas. When Chief Joseph's band was finally driven from their homes in 1877, their large horse herd was estimated to be from one-third to one-half Appaloosas. These horses proved their worth that summer as for thirteen hundred miles they outmarched and out-fought four armies before they finally were surrounded and captured in northern Montana.

Just before the war Chief Joseph had a war horse, Ebenezer, so famous that the Walla Walla newspaper mentioned him in the local column when Chief Joseph rode the spotted stallion into town.   *

*   Drawing and above quote, Courtesy *Redwood Empire Appa-loosa 1970 Yearbook.*

Chapter 7

CHIEF JOSEPH: THE MAN WHO DIDN'T WANT WARS

The name given to Joseph by his people was In-mut-too-yah-lat-lat, which meant Thunder-Traveling-Over-the-Mountain. Chief Joseph's statement, when he consented to give up his homeland and move to a reservation, shows the kind of man he was. *"I said in my heart that, rather than have war, I would give up my country. I would give up everything rather than have the blood of the white men upon the hands of my people."* The Nez Perce had always been at peace with the white man. These were the people who had treated the Lewis and Clark expedition with great kindness and hospitality.

In 1834, Captain Bonneville visited the Nez Perce, and in his report said, *"They were friendly in their dispositions, honest to the most scrupulous degree in their intercourse with the white man."* Further commenting on the Nez Perces, he said, *"Simply to call these people religious would convey but faint idea of the deep hue of piety and devotion which pervades their whole conduct. Their honesty is immaculate, and their purity of purpose and their observance of the rites of their religion are most uniform and remarkable. They are certainly more like a nation of saints than a horde of savages."*

When asked by the commission about bringing schools onto the Wallowa Reservation, Joseph replied, *"No, we do not want schools, for they will bring churches."* *"Why don't you want churches?"* asked the commissioner. *"Because they will teach us to quarrel about God, as the Catholics and Protestants do on the other Nez Perce Reservation; and at other places. We do not want to learn that. We may quarrel with men sometimes about things on this earth. But we never quarrel about God. We do not want to learn that."*

Chief Joseph, the famous and well-loved leader of the Nez Perce.
Photo taken in 1877.
                Courtesy *Bureau of American Ethnology.*

At the time when Joseph's father was dying, he called his son to him. Chief Joseph tells of it. *"My father sent for me. I saw he was dying. I took his hand in mine. He said, 'My son, my body is returning to my Mother Earth, and my spirit is going very soon to see the Great Spirit Chief. When I am gone, think of your country. You are the chief of these people. They look to you to guide them. Always remember that your father never sold his country. You must stop your ears whenever you are asked to sign a treaty selling your home. A few years more and the white man will be all around you. They have their eyes on your land. My son, never forget my dying words. This country holds your father's body. Never sell the bones of your father and mother.' I pressed my father's hand and told him I would protect his grave with my life. My father smiled and passed away to the spirit land."*

"I buried him in that beautiful valley of winding water. I love that land more than all the rest of the world. A man who would not love his father's grave is worse than a wild beast."

After meeting with the Indian commission in 1873, the commissioners were so impressed that they petitioned President Grant, and he issued an executive order setting aside the Wallowa Valley for the Nez Perce. But then in 1875 at the insistence of Governor Grover, he rescinded this order, taking the land again away from the Nez Perce.

The Nez Perce were divided into the Upper and Lower bands. The Upper Band had accepted and signed the treaty because their chief was friendly and agreeable to the government. The government made him head chief of the Nez Perce. This chief was called Lawyer. The government claimed they had made a treaty for the Lower Nez Perce band's land as well.

Joseph and the Lower Nez Perce accepted no treaty goods. When the commission said that the Indians had sold the Wallowa Valley, Chief Joseph's reply was, *"Suppose a white man should come to me and say, 'Joseph, I like your horses. I want to buy them.' I say to him, 'No, my horses suit me; I will not sell them.' Then he goes to my neighbor and says to him, 'Joseph has some good horses. I want to buy them but he refuses to sell.' My neighbor answers, 'Pay me the money and I will sell you Joseph's horses.' The white man returns to me and says, 'Joseph, I have bought your horses and you must let me have them.' If we sold our lands to the government, this is the way they bought it."*

General Howard gave the Nez Perce only 30 days to gather their stock and horses for removal to Lapwai Reservation. Yet Joseph prepared to move to avoid bloodshed. He knew that he couldn't hope to defeat the United States and that fighting would only result in slaughter of his people.

The Indians had been mistreated by the whites who had come in and stolen horses and cattle belonging to the Nez Perce. They had branded young stock belonging to the Indians. Indians had been murdered by whites and there was no recourse or justice left to the Indians.

Two Indians had been tied up and beaten by white ranchers. Yet Joseph preached peace and restraint to his people.

Now Chief White Bird's people were gathered together in camp with Joseph's. Joseph was away from camp, and the young men were gambling and talking wild. What of beatings and cheating by the whites? Should the Nez Perce put up with this any more? Three of them rode out and killed the rancher who had beaten them up.

Now all restraint was gone. They killed three more whites and then returned to camp, boasting of their experience. *"Look now. Here is war. There can be no more waiting."* Others joined them and they went out and killed more people who had wronged and cheated them.

When Joseph returned to camp, it had been done. There was no stopping now. Soldiers would come to punish them. Now Joseph schooled his men for battle. Less than half had guns. But the Nez Perce were to prove themselves outstanding marksmen.

Now Joseph showed his generalship. If he must fight, then he would pick the battlefield. He moved his people to White Bird Canyon, and there waited for the troops.

General Howard, on hearing the news, ordered out Colonel Perry with 90 men to punish the Indians and herd them onto the reservation. Joseph, who had never fired a gun in anger against the white man, was not to be taken by surprise. He carefully hid his men for ambush. Others he placed on horseback in a side canyon. These, Perry's men rode past. In spite of his Indian scouts, he rode straight into the trap. Joseph had Perry's troops surrounded on three sides. At Joseph's signal, the Nez Perce sharpshooters opened up. Troopers fell from their saddles. Then Joseph's men charged. Perry tried to retreat. At the same time, Joseph's mounted horsemen charged from the side canyon. The retreat became a rout.

Seventeen men under the leadership of a Lieutenant Theller rode into a blind draw. For the Nez Perce, it was like a shooting gallery. Not one of the troops came out alive. Now Joseph knew he could no longer stay on in that area. He began his famous 1200 mile trek with women and children and all their livestock, doubling back and forth using all their Indian skills. They passed through high mountain passes on what was thought of as an impossible journey.

During this time, the Army had 2000 troops in the field, plus other volunteer groups. Joseph's band, in the next 3½ months, fought 17 engagements. Yet they conducted themselves outstandingly. They did no scalping, and when they took women prisoners, they were treated with respect. They bought and paid for supplies at trading posts often at excessively high prices, and on occassion, gave water to a wounded enemy. After reaching the Bear Paw Mountains in Montana, Joseph felt that they were safe. Here they camped less than thirty-five miles from the Canadian border -- a chance for their wounded to recover and to rest their weary people and livestock.

Here they were attacked by troops commanded by General Miles. The Nez Perce, though weakened by long months of travel and fighting, rallied and drove the troops off with great loss to the troops. The Nez Perce worked all night digging trenches and preparing fortifications.

The next morning, Miles sent a half breed scout under a flag of truce asking to see Joseph. When they met, Miles demanded unconditional surrender. Joseph refused. He said he was willing to return to his homeland and there live in peace.

Miles now ordered a twelve pound cannon used against the Indians. But rather than panicking, the Nez Perce remained cool, firing accurately and keeping the troops pinned down with their fire. That evening Miles again demanded Joseph's surrender. *"The war is over. You must give up your guns."* *"We can only give up half of them,"* Joseph replied. *"We need guns for hunting and food."* *"No,"* said Miles. *"I must have them all and when I return you to Idaho, I will give them back, and your horses, and the government will help you to live."*

Joseph was willing to surrender, but first, he had to talk to his people. While Joseph was being held by the General in conference, the Nez Perce kept a Lieutenant hostage. He tried to get them to surrender their guns to him, but they refused. The Nez Perce didn't agree on surrendering, and so the fighting went on. Joseph's band could have escaped to Canada, but they would not leave their wounded and women and children. They had never heard of a wounded Indian recovering in the hands of the white man.

On October 5th General Howard arrived, and he immediately sent a Nez Perce scout who had come from Lapwai Reservation to offer Joseph new terms to surrender. Joseph came out to parley, and he told how it went. *"General Miles said to me, 'If you will come out and give up your arms, I will spare your lives and send you back to the reservation.' I do not know what happened between Miles and Howard I could not bear to see my wounded men and women suffer any longer. We had lost enough already. I believed General Miles, or I never would have surrendered. I would have held him in check until my friends came to my assistance. (He was expecting help from Sitting Bull.) And then neither the generals nor the soldiers would have left Bear Paw Mountain alive."*

On October 6th, after almost four months of fighting, Joseph's small brave band surrendered. Hear his speech; this is no *"Ugh-grunt"* stereotype Indian speaking: *"Tell General Howard that I know his heart. What he told me before I have in my heart. I am tired of fighting. Our chiefs are killed. Looking Glass is dead. Too-hul-hul-sute is dead. The old men are all dead. It is the young men who now say yes or no. He who led the young men is dead, (Joseph's brother, Alokut). It is cold and we have no blankets. The little children are freezing to death. My people, some of them, have run away to the hills and have no blankets and no food. No one knows where they are. Perhaps freezing to death. I want to have time to look for my children and see how many of them I can find. Maybe I shall find them among the dead. Hear me, my chiefs, my heart is sick and sad. From where the sun now stands I shall fight no more against the white man."*

After the surrender, Joseph had only 79 warriors. Of these, 46 were wounded. I should like to be able to say that the Nez Perce were returned to their reservation according to what was promised them. But no, the forked tongue of that white man in Washington came into play again.   Instead, they were moved to the Tongue River in Montana, and then to Bismarck, North Dakota, and finally to Leavenworth, Kansas, where many of them sickened and died. General Miles was opposed to this breaching of his word by Washington, but this didn't stop it. After that they were moved to the Indian Territory where they were offered some sagebrush and sand for a permanent reservation.

Joseph made trips to Washington asking to be returned to his land. All of this was received by Washington's official deaf ears. In 1879, an interview with Joseph was published in the North American Review. His concluding statement was, *"Let me be a free man, free to travel, free to stop, free to work, free to trade where I choose, free to choose my own teachers, free to follow the religion of my fathers, free to talk, think and act for myself, and I will obey every law or submit to the penalty."*

In 1881, the government decided to return the Nez Perce to Idaho, that is, the survivors of Looking Glass and White Birds' bands. But Chief Joseph and his people were sent to Colville Reservation in Washington. There the missionaries were disturbed over Joseph having two wives. Joseph told them, *"I fought through the war for my country and these women. You took my country; I shall keep my wives."* Chief Joseph died and was buried at Nespelem, Washington.

Looking Glass, killed in battle in 1877, he was a chief whose loss was felt badly by Chief Joseph. Photo taken in 1871.

Courtesy *Bureau of American Ethnology*

Chapter 8

RED CLOUD

Red Cloud belonged to the Oglala Division of the Teton Sioux. Miners and hunters had been coming into the Sioux country for some time, and Red Cloud's people had always either driven them out or killed the invaders.

In 1866, the federal government asked for a peace council with the Sioux. This was to be held at Fort Laramie. But at the same time, the government had ordered Colonel Henry Carrington to the Powder River country. He was to construct forts along the Bozeman Trail. These forts, deep in the Sioux territory, would be a direct violation of Sioux rights. Here, before the treaty meeting even began, the white man was getting ready to break his word.

When Red Cloud saw the Colonel there with all his soldiers, he jumped up at the peace council and said, *"My people came to this place to talk peace, but the white eagle is not here for peace; you cannot talk peace with so many soldiers. I say he is here to steal the country of our fathers, and to build an iron trail for the fireboat which walks on mountains and frightens away our game. If this is so, there is no reason for more empty words; if it is so, my people will fight."* Thus Red Cloud described the railroad and locomotive. He wanted nothing of this smog-producing engine going through his country and driving out game. He referred to Colonel Carrington as the silver eagle because of the insignia on his shoulder.

The peace commissioners had nothing to offer. Red Cloud saw the truth and left.

In July, 1866, Colonel Carrington found a location for construction of Fort Phil Kearney. Red Cloud assembled his warriors. He began a harrassing action against the troops. Whenever a detail left the main body of troops, they were attacked.

The fort construction went on in spite of Red Cloud's efforts. The fort sent out logging crews under heavy guard, but during this time, Red Cloud's braves ran off almost all the post's horses and livestock.

On the morning of December 21, a wood cutting detail was under attack. Captain Fetterman asked to lead a relief force. He told Colonel Carrington, *"Give me eighty men and I'll ride through the whole Sioux nation"*.

Colonel Carrington gave him permission to relieve the wood train, *"But on no account pursue them beyond the Lodge Trail Ridge. Do you understand?"* *"Yes, sir. I shall obey your orders,"* said Captain Fetterman.

Red Cloud called back his warriors when he saw the relief force. The wood train gathered up their wounded and dead and beat a hasty retreat toward the fort. Captain Fetterman and his 80 men rode to the top of Lodge Trail Ridge. Red Cloud had concealed most of his men behind timber and in the gullies, and all Captain Fetterman saw was a few Indians daring him to fight.

Red Cloud had picked his strategy well. The Captain fell for it. He had boasted that with eighty men he would ride through the whole Sioux nation. Now he disobeyed a direct order and charged over the ridge. He was going to teach those Sioux a lesson. But once he was down in the valley, Red Cloud's men moved in, closing out his retreat.

Captain Fetterman's command lasted less than an hour, for Sioux came charging out of every gully. Every man was dead. The scalps of the pony soldiers hung on the belts of the Sioux braves.

Hearing the firing, Colonel Carrington ordered Captain Ten Eyck out to support Captain Fetterman. He took 54 men and rode out. He went to the top of the ridge. Down below, the valley was full of Sioux warriors. They shook their weapons and challenged them to fight. Captain Ten Eyck saw there were too many Sioux and sent a messenger back to the fort for a cannon and more reinforcements. There weren't enough horses or mules left to pull the cannon, as the Indians had driven off so much stock.

But Colonel Carrington dispatched forty more troopers to help Captain Ten Eyck's men. By now there were no Indians left in the valley. So Captain Ten Eyck went ahead to see what had happened. He found Captain Fetterman and 49 of his men. They had been beaten out of their saddles in close combat. Some had taken cover behind boulders, but to no avail. Captain Fetterman and Captain Brown had powder burns on their heads. They had killed themselves rather than face capture by the enraged Sioux.

The Sioux left to make a council on attacking and destroying the whole fort. Red Cloud was determined to drive the white invaders from his people's land. The Colonel was really afraid of attack on the fort.

Carrington went out the next day to find the rest of Fetterman's command. He found them. They had met with the same fate as the others.

Some historians refer to the Fetterman fight as a massacre. It was really a military defeat. But since the Indians won, the white men called it a massacre. Fetterman had disobeyed a direct order. He let his arrogance lead him into doing something stupid.

Red Cloud would have attacked the fort that winter, but heavy blizzards set in and the Indians went into winter camp. The winter was the time to stay in camp, find a good sheltered place, and live out the winter. Besides, in the winter the Sioux spread out into many small camps. That way they could get deer and small game in their surrounding areas.

In June the next year, Red Cloud's warriors renewed the harrassment of the troops. Mostly hitting small groups, the Indians felt that if they kept it up, the government would pull out of their country.

The fort sent out a wood cutting detail. They took the heavy wagon boxes off the wagons and set them on the ground. They had sent out 28 men to guard the detail. But unknown to Red Cloud, these men were armed with Springfield repeater rifles. These were the first that had been used by troops. Red Cloud's men were armed with bows and arrows, lances, and a few single shot rifles that had been taken from troopers or bought in trade.

Red Cloud expected to lose a few men in the first assault. His men were brave, and brave men have always fought for their homes and families. He deployed his warriors to attack in waves from all sides so as to spread the fire of the defense as thin as possible. At first they crept forward through the bushes and rocks so as to get as close as they could before charging.

The soldiers under Captain Powell held their fire until the Indians were almost upon them. Then they fired. Many braves fell by the first gunfire. Yet they kept coming. Only at the wagon box corral did they stop.

The troopers stood up to fire. Red Cloud thought there were more soldiers in the wagon boxes than he had counted on. He dismounted his warriors and had them concentrate the fire of what guns they had, and then charge on foot. But again they were met with the heavy gunfire of the repeaters. They pressed on in spite of casualties, but to no avail. Red Cloud's men made one more mounted charge. But seeing that it was impossible to overcome the white man's fortress, he called a retreat.

Still the Indians had to remove their dead and wounded from the battlefield. No Indians would be left for the white man souvenir hunters to take the heads from and bleach out the skulls and claim *"this was the skull of an Indian who died in the wagon box fight."* And to leave the wounded for the tender mercy of the soldiers was unheard of. So while his warriors concentrated their fire on the white man's wagon box fort, other braves dragged off the wounded and dead.

Now a relief force arrived from the fort, and they fired cannons at the Indians. Red Cloud withdrew his forces.

In spite of their losses, Red Cloud was able to keep the Sioux interested in keeping the fort and surrounding area under harrassment. No soldiers dared venture out alone, and all livestock had to be kept under close watch. Finally the United States asked for another peace council with the Sioux. Red Cloud demanded they leave all their forts and get out of Sioux country. There could be no peace as long as the invaders remained.

The treaty read, *"The country north of the North Platte and east of the summits of the Big Horn Mountains shall be held and considered to be unceded Indian territory. No white person or persons shall be permitted to settle upon or occupy any portion of the same; or without the consent of the Indians, first had and obtained, to pass through the same; that all military posts be left."* And only when the troops had been withdrawn would Red Cloud sign the treaty.

Red Cloud had won. The soldiers pulled down their flag and left the fort. They were only a short distance away when Red Cloud's warriors set the fort on fire. This was the last fighting that Red Cloud did. Even during the Custer fight and other battles, he did not go. He lived on among his people, a great counselor and source of wisdom. Yet during his early life, he was foremost in battle. He killed a hundred and seventeen men in battles, according to a Sioux historian.

I know Red Cloud's grandson and great grandson, and they take deep pride in their heritage. They are both good Indian dancers and know much of their history. They live south of Rapid City, South Dakota. As they would say, Wash-tay! It is good!

I have told the story of Red Cloud.

Red Cloud, Chief of Pine Ridge Agency, South Dakota (in his prime).
Courtesy *South Dakota State Historical Society.*

Chapter 9

PONTIAC, THE OTTAWA

Pontiac saw the arrogance of the British, and that they were unlike the French who came to live with the Indians, trading with them, and asking for only enough ground to build their trading posts. But the British allowed their settlers to push beyond the boundaries set by the tribes, and any appeals to remove the settlers were not accepted by the Crown or its local governors.

When the French had the posts and forts, the Indians came to them in time of hunger and need, and the French commanders gave them provisions and guns and ammunition for their hunting. The French traders would come to their camps and supply them there, saving long trips into different trading posts.

Now, with the defeat of the French, all this was changed. The proud British treated the Indians like dirt in their own lands.

Pontiac planned to unite all the tribes against the British. He traveled from tribe to tribe with the wampum belt of war, asking the Indians to take up the hatchet against the British. He was a tremendous orator, and when a tribe found out that he was going to speak, Indians came from all over to hear him. He reminded them of the wrongs they had suffered at the hands of the British.

Where he couldn't go personally, chiefs who had heard him would take up his cry. Across thousands of miles of wilderness, he built his armies. These would not be just hit and run raids. This would be an organized, perfectly-timed action. In the month of May, eleven of the twelve British forts would be attacked. Pontiac had leagued tribes from the east coast all the way to present-day Minnesota and Iowa, and down to Choctaw country. Many of these tribes were enemies, but they put aside their intertribal rivalry to fight in the Pontiac Confederacy against the British. There were Chippewa, Sauk and Fox, Winnebago, Miami, Wea, Kaskaskia, Mascouten, Piankashaw, Kickapoo, Shawnee, Delaware, Potawatomi, and Hurons besides his own tribe, the Ottawa.

The Ottawas were used to traveling between other tribes. Many of them were go-between traders with the French, buying goods from the French and re-trading to more distant tribes.

During the fifteen years of the French and Indian wars, the Ottawas fought on the side of the French, and Pontiac saw plenty of action. Pontiac was a man of great intelligence. He was a natural born leader. He could sway the mass to his thinking. He was a man who took pride in himself and his people. He would have been a leader and an asset to any race.

Pontiac expected help from Spain and France if he needed it, since they were fighting England, and France still held the Louisiana Territory. He believed in using whatever action was necessary. If deceit or ambush would wipe out the British, that was it. He learned war, and there was nothing nice about it.

The British were given the same courtesy that they gave the Indians. They said that the only good Indian was a dead Indian, and Pontiac felt the same about Englishmen. Yet the French and French Canadians were given complete freedom, and Pontiac gave strict orders that none of them or their property was to be molested.

Pontiac planned to take Detroit by strategy. His men had sawed off the barrels on their guns, and he took sixty chiefs and sub chiefs and asked entrance to the post. Their tomahawks and guns were concealed under their blankets. But the post commander, Major Henry Gladwin, had been warned, and all his officers and men were heavily armed. So when Pontiac was allowed to enter, he saw that the British troops were prepared, and realized that his plot had been betrayed. Some say that an Indian woman who was in love with the British commander told him. Others say it was one of the French Canadians who saw the Indians cutting off their guns and told the British of the attack. Pontiac was to give the signal by turning over a wampum belt as he offerred it to the commander. But seeing the ready state of the

British, Pontiac didn't do it.

Seeing nothing could be done, Pontiac spoke out against the British for having such a show of arms and unfriendliness. And then he led his chiefs and people back to camp. His warriors criticized him for not giving the signal to attack. So, the next day he led his delegation back across the river taking 65 canoes.

But this time, Commander Gladwin refused to admit the whole delegation. He said he didn't think the young braves needed to be at the council. Pontiac said that all his people wanted to smell the smoke of the peace pipe, and that if all of them weren't allowed in, then none would go. Seeing that he couldn't gain entrance to the fort, Pontiac returned to his camp and announced that the war would begin. They would kill all the English outside the fort and then lay siege to the fort.

Now his braves surrounded the fort. But good news was coming into Pontiac's camp from other areas. On May 16, a combined force of Hurons and Ottawas surprised the English at Fort Sandusky on Lake Erie and captured or killed everyone there, and five boat loads of supplies, destined for Fort Detroit, instead were now in the camps of the Indians.

On May 25 the Potawatomis took Fort St. Joseph in northern Michigan, then Fort Miami fell. Pontiac's warriors had penetrated into what is now the State of Indiana. Fort Pitt, at the present site of Pittsburg, was under siege. General Amherst, who regarded the Indians as being docile and afraid of the English, was having to revise his idea of the Indians. How could this be happening?

Then Fort Ouiatenon fell to a war party of Kickapoos and their allies. Now the Chippewa organized a ball game of lacrosse at Fort Michilimackinac. They had previously given their weapons to their women to hold, and they were standing up against the walls of the fort, the sawed-off muskets and tomahawks concealed under their blankets. The commander of the fort had opened the gates for his troops to watch the game. Then a brave threw the ball and it went into the fort. Both teams charged after it, and as they came to their women, they got their weapons.

The British died to the last man, while the French who were at the fort were spared. The Chippewa lost not a man. Such was the success of their Trojan Horse technique.

The Senecas and Shawnee wiped out Fort Venango in Pennsylvania. Fort Le Boeuf was wiped out. And then Fort Presqu'Isle was destroyed by a combined force of Indians. At Fort Edward Augustus near Green Bay, Wisconsin, the British just packed up and left. Now only Fort Detroit and Fort Pitt held out against the Indians.

Certainly Sir Amherst, the smart commander-in-chief of the British, had underestimated the Indian forces under Chief Pontiac. Britain might rule the seven seas, but one particular Indian had stopped all their shipping on the Great Lakes. General Amherst had doubled the reward which was offered for the death of Pontiac.

Pontiac was a good friend to the French, and to one man in particular whose name was Baby. He stayed overnight there with Pontiac. Pontiac knew the British had offered him a reward for betraying him, but he knew the man wouldn't accept.

Another time a French Canadian complained to Pontiac that Indians were stealing from him. Pontiac camped there that night, and caught the thieves and drove them off, giving them a good scolding.

Now the British commander-in-chief realized the seriousness of things. He sent Captain James Dalzell to collect an army in New York and to go to the relief of Fort Detroit. He marched with 260 men and then went by boat on Lake Erie, coming into the fort under cover of fog, thereby making it safely to the fort. Young Dalzell now told Gladwin, the fort commander, that he intended to attack Pontiac's camp. Gladwin didn't entirely agree with the young captain. But he let him go.

But Pontiac had prepared an ambush for him. Pontiac let him march out with his 260 men. He got out 2 miles from the fort, and there, at a bridge, Pontiac hit him. When he tried to retreat, his rear was under attack, and behind some piles of cord wood, more of Pontiac's men waited. Dalzell was trapped. Then Pontiac ordered a charge. The captain was shot dead, but about two hundred of his men made it back to the fort.

But things were changing. The French had signed a treaty with Britain. The siege of Fort Pitt was broken.

It's interesting to note that the civilized British General Amherst suggested that blankets be infected with smallpox and given to the Indians in order to destroy them. Nice people! No wonder Pontiac and the Indians felt as they did about them. The Indians were not used to long sieges, and with the news of France making peace with England, and with no provisions to carry on the fight, the tribes, one by one, left Pontiac, made their separate peace with the British and went out to hunt. After all, they needed food for their families for the winter.

Thus ended Pontiac's dream of driving out the invaders and returning the land to the Indians. Still he tried to rally the tribes for the next two years. But there was no chance. The British peace-makers were now hard at work. They bought the chiefs with trade goods or cowed them with threats of troops.

Finally in April, 1769, Chief Pontiac was struck down by a jealous Indian for some reason -- perhaps hoping to gain glory by slaying the great chief. But Pontiac is remembered in history as a man who shook the British Lion and fought hard for his people and the things he believed in.

Plenty Coups, taken in the year 1880.
   Courtesy *Bureau of American Ethnology Collection.*

Chapter 10

LOGAN, A CHIEF OF THE MINGOES

The Mingoes lived in what is the present State of Ohio. Logan had always counseled his people to peace with the white man. He was a man of extreme honesty.

One time a frontier woman was saying how she wished she had a pair of moccasins for her little daughter, as she needed more support in walking. Soon Logan dropped by and asked if he might take the child to visit him. At first, she was fearful to let her child go with the Indian. But she let him take her. It wasn't till nightfall that they returned with her daughter wearing a pair of beaded moccasins which Logan had made himself for her.

During the French and Indian Wars and the Pontiac uprising, Logan held his people at peace, and they spoke of him as the friend of the white man. There had been some incidents that the settlers blamed on the Indians. But there were plenty of lawless whites and it was more likely that they were responsible. So, with nothing to go on but his hatred of Indians, in the spring of 1774, Captain Cresap gathered together a band of eager killers and they pounced on the first handy Indians. The Indians were Logan's family, camped at Yellow Creek, and they were murdered. Logan had been away at a peace council where he had persuaded the tribe to agree to peace with the white man. And on his return, Logan found his reward for being kind to the white man.

Now Logan was foremost in war. He took a war party of eight or ten warriors and went out and killed and drove the settlers out of the border settlements. Logan's band had captured a white man and were going to torture him at the stake. Logan argued in vain for the man's life. Then, when they had him tied, Logan leaped among them and placing a wampum belt around the prisoner's neck, said, *"I claim him as my brother to replace the one killed at Yellow Creek."* Such was the courage of Logan.

Later, Logan dictated a message and had it attached to the handle of a war axe that was driven into the wall of a cabin where they had killed the settlers. It read, *"Captain Cresap: What did you kill my people at Yellow Creek for? The white people killed my kin at Conestoga a great while ago, and I though nothing of that. But you killed my kin again on Yellow Creek, and took my cousin prisoner. Then I thought I must kill too, and I have been three times to war since; but the Indians are not angry. Only myself. /signed/John Logan"*.

Now an army of 3000 men was raised by Lord Dunmore, governor of Virginia. He sent 1500 men by a northern route under General Andrew Lewis. Governor Dunmore was to lead the other army of 1500 himself. And they would meet at Point Pleasant, Ohio, and there fight the Indians.

General Lewis' army engaged Cornstalk, the Shawnee, and Logan's band. The Indians fought back well, with their leaders exhorting them to be brave. For awhile it looked as though the Virginians would be defeated. But the Indians were pushed back to some fallen timbers that they had arranged for fortifications. There they held until General Lewis sent some men behind them. Thinking that these were reinforcements from Lord Dunmore, the Indians retreated. At this, Dunmore sent a messenger telling General Lewis to cease from further battles.

Lewis still insisted on pursuing the Indians. So the governor came up and threatened to run him through with his sword if he didn't obey. The governor then sent a messenger to the Indians offering them peace.

Cornstalk and the other chiefs agreed to come into the peace conference. But Logan refused to attend. Governor Dunmore sent a messenger to Logan to find out his intentions since Logan was a powerful chief and could easily lead men on the warpath again.

Logan sent his reply and the governor read it in council before the whole frontier army, including Colonel Cresap. Here it is:

"I appeal to the white man to say if he ever entered Logan's cabin

*and he gave him no meat; if ever he came cold and naked and he cloth-
ed him not. During the course of the last long and bloody war (the
French and Indian War and the Pontiac fight) Logan remained idle in
his camp, an advocate for peace. Such was my love for the whites
that, my countrymen pointed as I passed and said, 'Logan is the friend
of the white man.' I had even thought to have lived with you, but
for the injuries of one man. Colonel Cresap, the last spring, in cold
blood and unprovoked, murdered all the relations of Logan, not even
sparing my women and children. There runs not a drop of my blood
in the veins of any living creature. This called on me for revenge. I
have sought it. I have killed many. I have fully glutted my vengeance.
For my country I rejoice at the beams of peace; but do not harbor a
thought that mine is the joy of fear. Logan never felt fear. He will
not turn on his heel to save his life. Who is there to mourn for Logan?
Not one."*

Thomas Jefferson and others spoke of and compared his speech to
that of the great Greek orators, and I agree with them. Logan lived
on and acted as a peace representative for his people at future times.
But his grief stayed with him to his death.

Red Jacket. (Shagoie watha' or He who causes them to be awake.)
Noted orator and chief. Born 1756, probably at Canoga, Seneca Co.,
N.Y. Died 1830, vicinity of present Buffalo, N.Y.

From the lithograph published by McKenney and Hall.

Cornplanter. (Gaye twahgeh, 'where it is planted' [?]) Also known
as John O'Bail. Born 1732-40. Died 1836.

From a lithograph published by McKenney and Hall.

Chapter 11

MANGUS COLORADO

This powerfully built man was six feet five inches tall. Besides being a man of great strength, he possessed great intelligence. He was an outstanding leader of the Apache people. He became a hard-hitting war chief, fighting across Arizona, Texas, and New Mexico, and down into Mexico.

But what drove him to the warpath? He belonged to the band of Mimbreno Apache who were living peacefully with their Mexican neighbors at the village of Santa Rita. These Mexicans were miners, and the Apaches allowed them to live in their territory. But the government of Chihuahua had passed a law paying a bounty on Apache scalps.

A group of seventeen American trappers under James Johnson decided that here was some quick money. So they made a deal with the Mexicans at Santa Rita. They invited the Apaches to a great fiesta.

After the Apaches had eaten and the men were drunk on mescal, the Mexicans brought out bags of corn that they said were gifts. When the Apaches gathered around the corn, the Americans fired cannons into their midst. These cannons were loaded with nails and all sorts of scrap iron, broken up for that purpose. After this, Johnson and his men, along with the Mexicans, finished off many more unarmed Apaches.

Mangus Colorado did not trust the Mexicans who had invited the Apache to this so-called fiesta, and he would drink no mescal. But Juan Jose, the chief of the Apache band, got drunk and was in no condition to help his people. Four hundred Apaches died that day.

Mangus Colorado's two wives were among those who died. Knowing that there was nothing he could do at the time, he grabbed a small Apache child and ran to escape the slaughter.

Now his heart was black with revenge. The only thing that the Mexicans and Americans would understand was killing, and he would give it to them. The Apache closed off all traffic in or out of Santa Rita. Mangus called in and asked support from all the other bands of Apaches. The people of Santa Rita depended entirely on food and supplies that were brought in from Janos, and now they were cut off.

The Apaches attacked and wiped out a group of 23 American trappers. Johnson and his group of trappers decided to depart from Santa Rita. Here were the men who had slaughtered the formerly peaceful Apaches. The Apaches, under Mangus Colorado, attacked. Only a few of the trappers escaped. The Apaches found saddle bags full of the silver paid for the scalps of their people.

The people of Santa Rita were running low on supplies, and some of them wanted to send a strongly armed group to see what was holding up the supply trains. But others were afraid to send away so many men, for fear the Indians would attack. Finally it was decided that everyone would leave together. The trip would be at night. Everyone took all their possessions they could carry. Many were packing them on their backs. Mangus Colorado's scout watched them leave, and immediately a runner was dispatched to the chief.

Now was the time for revenge upon the murderers of Santa Rita. But Mangus Colorado let them get three days out, then he chose a valley that they had to pass through. There his warriors were concealed behind boulders and trees, on both sides and at each end. And there the tired caravan of 400 people stopped to rest. Then the Apaches hit them. The Mexicans who were armed shot back, but to no effect. The Apaches stayed well concealed. After the Mexicans saw there was no possibility of fighting their way out, they tried to escape, running in every direction. But the Apaches picked them off.

Mangus let the padre and a few others escape to tell other Mexicans to stay out of Apache territory, and to tell them that this was repayment for the treachery of Santa Rita.

Mangus Colorado kept up raids against the Mexicans, going deep into Mexico. When in 1846, the United States declared war on Mexico, Mangus Colorado and his people offered to help the United

States. They sold horses and mules to the army, and even offered to send their warriors along. At this time Americans could pass safely through Apache land as long as they were just passing through.

In May, John R. Bartlett, head of the Mexican boundary commission arrived in New Mexico, Mangus Colorado came to see him. He said, *"I've come to make peace with the new white chief. I have been watching your party many days on the trail. You should not travel in Sonora with so small a party. There are many bad Apaches who disobey Cochise and me, and they might attack you. So we watched you every day to see that no harm came to you. Today I come into Santa Rita and am told you will decide what country belongs to the United States and what belongs to Mexico. I know all about this, for I have talked with your General Kearny and your Colonel Cooke. My people want to be friends with your people, but I want to ask you the same question I asked them, and which they could not answer: Why cannot Apaches have some country of their own? This country where we have hunted for all time does not belong to the Mexicans. They cannot sell it to the United States. It belongs to Apaches. It is not right for either Americans or Mexicans to take our hunting grounds away from us."*

Bartlett wasn't able to give any reply to Mangus Colorado's speech. Bartlett told him that he should no longer fight with the Mexicans.

Later, two Mexican boys who were captives of the Apache, came and asked protection of Bartlett's camp. The Apache often took Mexican boys and raised them up as sons to replace children captured or killed by the Mexicans. So Mangus Colorado and his men came into the white mens camp. *"Why did you take our captives from us?"*

Bartlett told Mangus that he was told by his commanders in Washington to take all Mexican captives from the Apache whenever he could. This outright meddling in their affairs made the Apaches very angry. They finally accepted payment for the boys when they saw it was useless to try to get them back. (This was not a matter of morality on the part of the United States. In the south, great numbers of slave-owners held slaves whom they treated far worse than the Apaches treated their captives.)

An Apache warrior who came along to visit the camp was shot by one of Bartlett's men. When the warrior died, the Apache demanded the life of the murderer. The Americans told the Apaches he would be punished, but this would happen after a trial in Santa Fe. The Apache wanted it right there at camp where it happened. They suspected the American's double standard of justice – one kind for their own people and another for the Indians. Maybe they had heard reports of how it was with the Eastern tribes, how an Indian's word was not accepted in the white man's court. The Apache were growing weary of the white man's one-sided approach to justice, so they drove off the boundary commission's horses and the troops ended up leaving on foot.

Now for a while, Mangus Colorado and his people were left alone. But then the white men came in search of the yellow iron, gold, the thing that drives white men mad. Mangus Colorado knew of another place where there was rich gold, away from his people and their hunting grounds. He tried to get the white men to go there. But instead, being the type of Indian-haters they were, they pounced on him and tied him to a tree. One miner picked up a whip. Mangus warned them not to whip him, because no Indian would stand for the disgrace of being whipped.

But the arrogant miners went ahead and whipped him. When Mangus Colorado recovered from this treatment by these men, he had only hate for all the invaders. There could be no peace with men that had no respect for the Indian people.

Mangus Colorado's first action against the miners came about a month later. He let some Apache maidens be seen by the miners. They were gathering wood near the camp. The white men started out in eager pursuit of the girls. But after they got away from their camps, Mangus Colorado's Apache cut down the white men with bows and arrows and rifle fire.

Now Mangus Colorado and his warriors were constantly on the warpath. Cochise and Victorio joined with him in many battles. In 1861, California volunteers, commanded by Captain Thomas Roberts, were heading east to fight for the Union against the Confederacy. Mangus Colorado's scouts reported seeing the troops approaching Apache Pass. So Mangus ordered his braves to prepare an ambush. They waited until the soldiers were well inside the pass. Then Mangus gave the order to start firing. The soldiers were being fired on from all directions. But the Apaches kept so well concealed that to return the fire was useless.

Every boulder seemed to hide an Indian. Captain Roberts was forced to retreat, but he had to get through the pass. His group had marched all day and now they must get to water. He ordered his men into the pass again, only this time they watched carefully. But they still weren't able to make it through to the spring. Mangus Colorado's warriors had built fortifications and the troopers were not getting through.

Then Captain Roberts dispatched some men back to warn the supply train. Thinking that they might be going to get help, Mangus Colorado left warriors with Cochise to hold the pass and rode off in pursuit. One of the cavalry riders shot at the pursuing Indians and Mangus was hit. With their leader badly wounded, the Indians gave up the fight with the cavalry. This great leader's life was worth the lives of a hundred men. Now all thought was to save him.

They carried Mangus Colorado south to Mexico. They rode to the town of Janos. They told the Mexican soldiers that no harm would come to them or their town if they let them in to see the doctor.

This man, Mangus Colorado, was greatly loved by his people and his sub-chiefs. Now he was badly wounded and about to die. They brought him to a doctor who must remove the bullet. If the chief died, everyone in the town would die. The Apaches didn't trust the doctor, but they knew that with this threat over his head, he would do his best for their chief. There would be only the best of care. This was one wounded Indian who would live, and Mangus Colorado recovered. His strong body that was conditioned by tough outdoor living mended. His people took him onto a mountain retreat and nursed him back to health.

But Mangus knew that his people couldn't forever fight the white man. There were always more coming. He wanted a fair peace for his people. And when the army contacted him to make a peace parley, he was ready to respond. Cochise and other chiefs warned him that the white man might not be sincere, that this was a trick to capture him. But Mangus Colorado wanted to see peace for his people. So he went to the camp of Captain Shirland under a white flag of truce, a symbol that is supposed to be respected by all civilized people. But when he arrived in the camp he was immediately taken prisoner.

When Colonel West, the commanding officer of the area, heard of his capture, he rushed to the camp. He ordered two soldiers to guard him and their instructions were to make it look like he was trying to escape and then kill him.

In the night, one guard heated his bayonet red hot and placed it against the leg of the sleeping chief. When Mangus leaped up, both guards fired on him, killing him. Thus ended the life of a great Indian leader.

Mangus Colorado was able to organize and coordinate Indians from all over the area. He loved his people and worked hard for them. He was intelligent and would be a fine man for any people to remember. For this, we cherish his memory.

—*Charles Clayton*

Chapter 12

QUANAH PARKER, A MAN OF PEACE AND WAR

Quanah belonged to the band of Comanche known as Kwahadi, meaning Antelope-Eaters. His mother was Cynthia Ann Parker, a white captive. She was captured when she was nine years old -- on May 19, 1836. The Comanches raided Parker's Fort and took her and four other captives. Nakoni, the Comanche chief, took her as his wife. The Comanches being polygamists had more than one wife, so Quanah had many half sisters and half brothers.

Cynthia Ann was recaptured by the Texas Rangers in 1860. She had her small child Prairie Flower with her and tried desperately to outride the Texas Rangers. After living for many years the free life of the Comanches, she could not adjust back to life in the white man's world.

Her little daughter died soon after her capture, and Cynthia Parker, the Comanche white woman, would sit in grief and think of her husband and young sons riding free on the open plains. She died in 1864 heartbroken, unable to return to her family and those she loved.

Quanah grew to manhood and became a great leader of his people. When the other Comanche bands made treaty with the United States at Medicine Lodge in 1867, Quanah Parker led his people out on the Staked Plains. He hunted buffalo and antelope where he chose. This was the land of his people. When the white buffalo hunters and Texas Rangers pressed close, he fought back, and his warriors raided all over Mexico and Texas. But as band after band of Comanches went to the reservation, Quanah saw that the old life was over.

In 1875, a group of government peacemakers came in search of

Quanah Parker. Born: 1845. Died: 1911.
Bureau of American Ethnology Collection

Quanah. He listened to their treaty talk. Not all of it was to his liking. To be forced to live in one place on a reservation, to have to have government cards to go temporarily off the reservation, to have to ask anyone for permission for anything, was contrary to his free nature. But he wanted peace for his people. He was tired of having the Texas Rangers hunt his people like wild animals.

So on June 2,1875, Quanah Parker rode in at the head of his band consisting of one hundred warriors, 300 women, children, and old people, and 1500 horses. And at Fort Sill, then Indian territory, now Oklahoma, Quanah Parker gave up his arms and pledged his people to the ways of peace.

Quanah now set about learning the white man's ways. If his people must live with the white man, then he would lead them. He built a white man's house and went into ranching, and encouraged his people to do so as well. He counseled his people in learning from the white man, and fought to protect their rights. If he felt his people had been cheated or suffered injustice at the hand of the white man, he was there to speak up for them. Yet if they did wrong, he would turn them over to the white man's law. He wore the white man's clothing except at special ceremonial times when he put back on his Indian clothes.

When the army tried to recruit Quanah's men as scouts and soldiers, he refused to let them go. He said, *"We have made a peace treaty and the white missionaries say it is wrong to fight and kill. Therefore my people will not do this wrong."*

Quanah Parker is credited with being a peyote priest. He brought the peyote religion to his people and practiced it faithfully.

While visiting Washington, a Bureau of Indian Affairs official told Quanah that he could no longer practice polygamy, that to have more than one wife was not proper. He said, *"When you get back home, Quanah, pick out the wife you like best and tell the rest of them that they must get out."* Quanah listened but said nothing. So the official kept after him. *"Just pick out your favorite wife and tell the others they've got to move."* *"You tell 'em,"* said Quanah. And that ended the subject.

Quanah had his mother Cynthia Ann Parker's remains moved to the Indian territory, and his request was that he be buried alongside of her. Thus, in death, Cynthia Ann Parker was reunited with her warrior son. The inscription on Quanah's tombstone reads, *"Resting here until day breaks, and shadows fall, and darkness disappears is*

Quanah Parker

Last Chief of the Comanches".

In Texas there is a town that proudly bears the name of Quanah, in honor of this outstanding leader. He was a man of great integrity. Once he had placed his feet on the path of peace, he never turned back. His word was like a bond.

Chapter 13

COCHISE

Cochise was described as a man of about six feet. He was slender and well-muscled. He was a man of keen intelligence -- a mild mannered and even tempered man, yet a man of great strength. Because of his cunning and warfare skill, the soldiers called him The Serpent. He was a Chiricahua chief.

In 1860, Cochise and his people were at peace with the whites. He had given them permission to run a stagecoach line through his territory. Cochise and his people protected the stage line from *"Bronco Apaches"* which was the name given to outlaw bands that raided free from tribal groups. His people even gathered wood and sold it to the stagecoach station.

However, in October of 1869 a band of Bronco raiders swept down on the ranch of Johnny Ward and took a boy who was part Apache, but his mother was Mexican. When John Ward returned to his ranch, he at once rode out to Fort Buchanan and reported the raid.

The fort commander immediately dispatched troops under Lieutenant Bascom proceeded to Apache Pass and there he stopped at the stage station and informed the station manager, Mr. Wallace, that he was after Cochise. When Wallace asked why, he said Cochise and his raiders had stolen cattle and taken a boy from the Ward Ranch. Wallace replied that he knew Cochise and his people, that they were friendly and at peace.

But to Bascom, all Indians were alike, and the only good Indian was a dead Indian. Bascom insisted that he would talk to Cochise and make him surrender the boy. And so Wallace went to Cochise's camp. Cochise decided it would be best to come and try to explain some sense to this Lieutenant Bascom. He brought along his two younger brothers and four other young men.

Cochise tells in his own words of the meeting. *"Face to face we stood and this I saw; that there was not in his head that with which to make his eyes fair dealing. He was of the tontos* 'fools.'" He accused Cochise of stealing cattle and taking the boy. When Cochise denied it, Bascom would not believe him. Cochise sent out his men to search for the boy among the Bronco Apaches. But Bascom would have none of that. He said this was just a trick to give them time to escape.

Cochise and his men had come into Bascom's camp under a flag of truce. Now he made them prisoners and said he would hold them hostages until the boy was found and returned. That night Cochise, using a hidden knife, slit a hole in the tent where he and his men were held, and they escaped. But his men were quickly recaptured.

Now Cochise called his people together and decided it was time to fight the white men. First he sent his men to drive off the horses of the soldiers. Others attacked the stage and captured two white men. In other fighting Cochise took captives too. But Lieutenant Bascom would not negotiate with Cochise.

Cochise and his men now attacked a wagon train that was coming through Apache Pass, and captured three more prisoners. He again tried to secure the release of his men. By now Lieutenant Bascom had secured additional support in more troops under a Captain Irwin. Bascom's reply was, *"Release your prisoners and give up the boy."* Cochise could do nothing of the kind since he didn't have the boy. So he rode off. The Army executed the Indian prisoners, and the Apaches killed the white prisoners in retaliation.

Cochise saw no peace or honesty from the whites. So now his people took to the warpath. Nothing would pass through Apache country. They attacked and raided over the white country. Troops were sent against them but to no effect. This was the Apaches' own country. Cochise, who had tried so hard for peace, now fought the white men with everything he had.

The government sent in more and more troops. But the Apache avoided the large forces and hit from a bush, wiping out or stealing horses from them. The old timers would watch some snappy West

Point officer ride out with his patrol who was ready to fight every Apache in the Southwest. But they would say, *"Looks like more horses for Cochise."* And sure enough, the troops would come back walking. They never saw an Indian until their horses were stampeded and stolen. This was the way of Cochise.

Cochise was greatly respected by his people. They tell how one time two of his men betrayed an ambush by firing upon the Cavalry before the signal. The Cavalry was warned and escaped, and many Apache died in the fighting with the troopers. Cochise called the men before him and executed them himself. To all men who knew him, white or Indian, his word was always true.

The name Cochise meant *"like ironwood."* Cochise kept his word and honor, but he could find no white man to trust.

Then came along Tom Jeffords. He was trying to establish a stage line and deliver mail, and his route ran through Apache country. He lost many men to the Apache and decided that if his line was to continue, he had to come to some agreement with Cochise. So he got an Apache scout, one of the friendlies who lived on a reservation.

I guess the scout would only take him so far, and then pointed the way to Cochise's stronghold. So Jeffords went on alone from there. When he reached Cochise's camp, he unbuckled his gun belt and went to talk with Cochise. They talked for some time and Jeffords explained that his work was a peaceful one of only carrying mail. Cochise could see that the man was honest and he respected him for having the courage to come into his camp alone. Because Jeffords came with an honest heart and showed respect and spoke the truth, Cochise made an agreement. Jeffords' drivers and riders could pass freely through the Apache country.

Jeffords and Cochise saw each other much after this, and there came a time when they cut their wrists and became blood brothers. But the other white men were still regarded as enemies, for they showed no change of heart toward the Apache. Cochise saw what the white men did to the friendly Apaches.

These evil white men surprised a camp of Apaches who were camped near Fort Grant, and on April 30, 1871, murdered 128 men, women and children. In all fairness, I must report that Lieutenant Whitman who was in charge at Fort Grant was a good human being. He had assembled these Apaches there and was even giving them some work cutting hay for the Army so he could pay them extra rations. But the Indian haters around the frontier town of Tucson, Arizona Territory, were of another breed.

Cochise was contacted by General Gordon Granger. The intermediary was Vincent Colyer. He was a man who was much respected by the Indians. He had shown himself to be truly interested in helping to settle the Indian problems, and through his efforts, several hostile bands had come in.

When the General and Cochise talked, Cochise said, *"The sun has been very hot on my head and made me as in a fire; my blood was on fire, but now I have come into this valley and drunk of these waters and washed myself in them and they have cooled me. Now that I am cool I have come with my hands open to you to live in peace with you. I speak straight and do not wish to deceive or be deceived. I want a good strong lasting peace. When I was young I walked all over this country, east and west, and saw no other people than the Apaches. After many summers I walked again and found another race of people had come to take it. How is that?"*

"Why is it that the Apaches want to die, that they carry their lives on their fingernails? They roam over the hills and plains and want the heavens to fall on them. The Apaches were once a great nation; they are now but a few and because of this they want to die and so carry their lives on their fingernails. Many have been killed in battle. You must speak straight so that your words may go as sunlight into our hearts. Tell me, if the Virgin Mary has walked throughout all the land, why has she never entered the wigwam of the Apache? Why have we never seen or heard her? I have no father nor mother; I am alone in the world. No one cares for Cochise; that is why I do not care to live, and wish the rocks to fall on me and cover me up. If I had a father and a mother like you, I would be with them and they with me. When I was going around the world, all were asking for Cochise. Now he is here. You see him and hear him. Are you ready for peace. If so, say so. Speak, Americans and Mexicans. I do not wish to hide anything from you nor have you hide anything from me. I will not lie to you; do not lie to me."

Cochise said that his people did not want to go to anyplace, but to remain in their own country. He said he would never go to the Reservation in New Mexico. *"That is a long ways. The flies on those mountains eat out the eyes of the horses. The bad spirits live there. I want to live in these mountains. I have drunk of these waters and they have cooled me; I do not want to leave here."*

The General promised Cochise that he would be allowed to remain in his home country. But a little while later the changeable white men came out with a new order. All the Indians must be moved to the Tularosa Reservation. The white man had broken his word to Cochise and his people. But Cochise must keep his word to his people. He left the reservation and his people followed him into the mountains again.

The Apaches once again were on the warpath. Their raiders hit far and wide. General Howard was sent from Washington. President Grant wanted to know what was behind the Indian trouble. General Howard was told that the only white man that Cochise would trust and talk to was Tom Jeffords. So he contacted Jeffords.

Jeffords would only take Howard if he would go alone without soldiers. The General agreed to this, and they went to the Apache camp using only two Apache guides.

Cochise called a council and with his other sub chiefs they agreed to peace, but only on the condition that they be allowed to remain in their beautiful homeland. General Howard gave Cochise his word that it would be as he wished. He also asked that Tom Jeffords be made their Indian agent. This was also granted. Cochise's people kept their word and there was peace in the land between Cochise's band and the whites. The Apache worked at supplying hay and wood to the military.

When Cochise got sick and knew he was dying, he sent for his friend Jeffords to say farewell to him. Like many of our old timers, he knew the exact time he would die. He said to Jeffords, *"At ten o'clock tomorrow morning I will die."*

After Cochise died, the Indians buried him and rode their horses over his grave, back and forth. This way no white man souvenir hunter could come and dig it up, as has happened so often. Tom Jeffords knew the location, but he kept it to himself. So Cochise was laid to rest in his beautiful land that he loved.

But after his death, greedy white men pushed the government to move the Apache people again to the Tularosa Reservation, but many of them left the reservation and went on the warpath again.

Today many of Cochise's people raise cattle and yet there is much unemployment and hunger on their reservation. We wonder when the Great White Father in Washington will keep his promises to these and other Indian people. Maybe, sometime, we hope.

Chapter 14

OSCEOLA

Osceola was a half-breed being part Indian and part Scottish. He spent most of his boyhood among the Creek Indians, his mother's people. However the Creeks to whom he belonged were called Seminoles by the northern bands. This was because the Seminoles had left the northern groups and moved to Florida. The name Seminole means runaway.

Because his father was part white, he had an English name and was known as Billy Powell. But his Indian name given to him by his tribe was Osceola, meaning Black Drink Singer. This black drink ceremony was an important part of their tribal rites. Before a major council meeting their chiefs, or Tustenuggees, would drink great amounts of this drink to purify themselves. When the warriors prepared for the warpath they also drank the Black Drink.

The Seminoles tried to get along with the white man. But they were forced onto a reservation totally unfit for living and the food and provisions promised them never arrived. So they were forced to go outside of their reservation. This was in the year 1825.

At the same time the slave owners claimed the Seminoles were harboring runaway slaves and sent raiding parties in to take back the slaves, often taking free men and Seminoles as well. Then the United States' next move was to try and force the removal of all the Seminoles to the Oklahoma Territory.

They sent a delegation of six Seminole chiefs along with interpreters to look at the Oklahoma Territory and because of the suffering these people had in Florida, they agreed to resettle. But many of the

Osceola. (Asi-yaholo, or Black Drink Halloer). Born: 1803; died: 1838. A prisoner at Fort Moultrie, S. C.

From a portrait painted by George Catlin, 1838.

Florida Seminoles refused to be moved and they contended that these six chiefs were just a delegation to look at the land and that they were not bound by their decision. But the government would recognize only the chiefs who were in agreement to their treaty. And even some of the chiefs who had signed this document to relocate now refused, claiming it was a fraud and had been misrepresented to them.

Now the government demanded that all the Indians be removed to Oklahoma or the Indian Territory as it was known then. Osceola, who in the past had tried to get along with the whites, had even been a reservation policeman under Chief Micanopy, head chief of the Seminoles, now became strongly opposed to the Americans and their deceptive ways of trying to force the Indian removal.

In October 1834, the military general of Georgia, Wiley Thompson, called a meeting of Seminole leaders at Fort King. Osceola there showed himself as a leader and statesman. He spoke out strongly a-gainst the removal. After more negotiations, General Clinch, the fort commander threatened to use troops to force their removal. For his resistance and refusal to comply, Osceola was arrested and some of the other chiefs were forced to sign an agreement to relocate. In order to gain his release, Osceola also was forced to sign. (It is interesting to note what nice methods this country used to take lands away from the natives. Maybe this is why so many other countries are getting fed up and are saying, *"Go home, Yankee dogs."*)

Later, in council with other chiefs, Osceola decided to refuse to honor the relocation order they were forced to sign. They also agreed that any chief who made preparations to relocate would be killed and they executed one. Now there would be resistance to the whites. The Seminoles prepared for battle. Arms were bought wherever possible. The Seminoles went into hiding in the swamps. Now they made hit and run raids against the settlements and soldiers. Osceola and his men were everywhere and other chiefs were leading their men on raids.

Jumper, another outstanding Seminole leader lead his band in daring raids often joining with Osceola. Hundreds of soldiers and settlers were being killed. Now all the pent-up hate for the past mis-treatment was being released.

Settlers who had led raids to take slaves and Indians into slavery were hunted down and killed. More Negro slaves fled from their masters and joined the Seminoles. Some of the Seminole strongholds were almost entirely Negro. Osceola led his men against the Indian agency on the reservation. They killed Wiley Thompson, who had forced Osceola to sign the agreement.

Meanwhile, other Seminoles under Jumper, Micanopy, and Alligator attacked two companies of troops under Major Francis Dade. The Seminoles wiped out almost the complete force. Only three men out of 102 escaped, while only three Indians were killed and a few wounded.

General Clinch now came to try his hand against the natives. He had a force of 800 men. Osceola let 200 of the soldiers cross over a stream and then attacked them. After fighting most of the day and making bayonet charges that only temporarily dispersed the Indians, General Clinch retreated out of the area with a loss of four men killed and 59 wounded. Osceola was wounded in the battle.

President Jackson ordered more troops into the area. The United States' policy at that time as always, was, if you can't solve a problem with a little force, just add more force. Major General Gaines first tried his hand without success. Then General Winfield Scott. But the Seminoles kept out of the way of major troop concentrations and instead hit small outposts and settlements.

The soldiers suffered from malaria and other sickness. In fact, more died of disease than of conflict with the Indians.

General Scott failed to remove or defeat the Seminoles and he was removed. After him, another came -- General Call. He also failed. During this time, much more Army equipment was lost.

Osceola and his people were tired of being chased. Micanopy, the head chief of the Seminoles, went in and made an agreement to migrate to the Oklahoma Territory. The Seminoles were to assemble at Tampa Bay. Osceola and his people came in. Osceola had been sick, suffering from malaria and was very tired and thin. But the Seminoles had hardly got into camp before the greedy slave catchers were there claiming Indians and Negros alike. General Jessup offered no protection to the Seminoles. Osceola and other chiefs escaped to their villages where many of their people still remained. Then Osceola returned and, bringing warriors with him, ordered Micanopy and the other Seminoles to return to the Everglades. Around 700 Seminoles joined him.

General Jessup of course blamed the whole thing on the Seminoles and ordered renewed fighting against them. Meanwhile some Seminole bands did relocate. They were herded onto boats and treated like cattle. Many of them died on the way. Starvation and sickness was rampant among them. The historical accounts remind me of the Jews being removed from the occupied countries and shipped to concentration camps during World War II. But the Great Spirit always repays people for their mistreatment of their fellow man. Today all around you is seen the repayment for the past. I'm only happy to see it. Non-Indians are beginning to show signs of making amends.

In the later part of 1837, armies were again sent against the Seminoles. In October of that year, Osceola sent word that he wished to talk peace. So he waited in his camp under a flag of truce. The Americans came to him but had some 200 armed men following at a distance. These surrounded the camp and Osceola and his people were seized under the flag of truce. Because of this treachery, many other Seminoles refused to come in and talk with the Americans. Many of the newspapers of the day spoke out against this action against Osceola. But the government gave no response to public opinion.

Osceola was imprisoned at Fort Moultrie near Charleston, South Carolina. Now locked up, he took sick. The Americans offered him a white doctor, but instead, he asked to be treated by one of his own people. But the time had come for Osceola to leave his people. Here, a young man, but a man of great wisdom and courage was about to die. He asked for his loved ones to be gathered around him and to dress in the way of his people. He shook hands with the post officers and bid farewell to his friends and chiefs of his tribe, and then lay back and died. The post doctor cut off Osceola's head and preserved it to keep as a souvenir.

The Indians of that time were supposed to be the uncivilized ones!

There are still bands of Seminoles living in Florida today. The descendants of those who refused to leave or surrender are the ones you see, and it is a beautiful sight to see them still dressing and living in the old way.

Gall, the Hunkpapa war chief who fought in the Battle of the Little Big Horn.

Courtesy *Bureau of American Ethnology.*

Chapter 15

POWHATAN AND THE INDIANS OF VIRGINIA

Sir Walter Raleigh, in 1584, arrived in Virginia and spoke of the natives as peaceful and friendly, and to quote, *"a more kind loving people could not be."* He carried on trade and barter with them.

Sir Richard Grenville visited the area the next year, 1585, and left over 100 men to form the colony of Roanoke. (Not discovering gold, all returned to England the next year.) While on an exploration trip in the surrounding country, they laid the groundwork for future relations with the Indians. A young Indian boy took a silver cup from one of the party. So the English reaction was *"at Aquascoquoc the Indians stole a silver cup wherefore we burnt the town and spoiled their corn, so returned to our fleet at Tocohon."*

So with this, Captain John Smith arrived, and with his followers, set up Jamestown colony. The Smith group of colonists were completely unsuited for their task of setting up a colony. They were gamblers, spendthrifts, and people who had never worked in their lives and didn't intend to. The New World, as they called it, was a place full of rich Indian tribes from whom you just stole gold. Up to that time the Spanish had been very successful at taking gold in South America. The Spanish stole the gold from the Incas and Aztecs and the English had tried their best to steal it from the Spanish ships, but the Spanish were heavily armed, and for some Englishmen, that was too dangerous a business. So why not steal it direct from the poorly armed Indians? If you look at early history, you'll note that practically all of the early explorers did a little piracy on the side. So with Smith's men not willing or capable of work, the colony was in tough shape.

Smith and Captain Newport therefore undertook to trade with the Indians with hatchets, beads and copper. The Indians were reluctant to trade. To quote an old historian *"finding that the natives scorned him as a famished man, offering a morsel of food as the price of his arms, he adopted a very common expedient of the time, using force where courtesy availed not,"* thus establishing free enterprise on American soil.

After the colonists threatened to destroy their village, the winter corn supply and kill a few Indians, the Indians agreed to sell corn to the Jamestown colony for beads, hatchets, and other trade goods. At this time Captain Smith told his men not to kill or destroy too many Indians or villages. The reason was that there wouldn't be anyone to grow corn for the lazy bums at the colony. Historians put this a little different in wording, but implied the same thing.

Captain Smith now undertook an exploration of the Chickahominy River. Some of his people believed this would lead them to a south sea shore tribe who would have gold. After traveling some sixty miles up stream, it became impossible for the larger boat to go farther. So Smith instructed his men to remain on the boat and not go ashore. Then, taking two other white men and two Indians as guides, he proceeded up the river until he came to some marshes.

Meantime his men back at the boat disregarded his orders and went ashore. They were attacked by Indians under Opechancanough, chief of the Pamaunkee and a brother of Powhatan. He captured one of their number and the rest fled back to the boat. Forcing this man to tell which direction Smith and the others had taken, he then killed the captive and went in pursuit of Smith's party.

They found the two Englishmen asleep by a canoe. They shot them and then went in search of Smith. When they found him they attacked, but Smith tied one Indian guide to his arm, using him as a shield, and used his gun so effectively that he killed three Indians and wounded several others.

Not wanting to risk the loss of more men, Opechancanough held back his men. Smith, trying to retreat to the canoe, sidestepped and was hopelessly mired up to his shoulders in the bog along with his Indian guide. So, standing in bog and getting cold, he became a smart man and decided to surrender.

The Indians pulled Smith out of the bog and built a fire, rubbing his numb limbs and restoring circulation. Trying to get along with the chief, Smith gave him his pocket compass and then gave him and the braves a lecture on its use and other scientific matters of the universe. The Indians seemed to enjoy this, but when he finished, they tied him to a tree and started stringing their bows for additional entertainment. However, Opechanacanough decided to take him back to the Indian camp instead.

At the camp Smith was well fed and treated with kindness. The Indians held a victory dance to celebrate Smith's capture, and because of being well fed, Captain Smith thought they were doing this, as he said, *"to fatten him up to eat him."* An Indian gave him a robe to keep warm.

One old man attempted to kill him because his son was killed by the colonists. The Powhatans then took Smith around to show him to the surrounding tribes. Smith gave his description of the Indian medicine man, or conjurer, as he called him. He was left seated in a large cabin on a mat, *"and presently came skipping in a great grim fellow all painted over with many snakes and weasel skins stuffed with moss, and all their tails tied together, so as they met on the crown of his head in a tassel, and round about the tassel was a coronet of feathers, the skins hanging round about his head, back and shoulders, and in a manner covered his face, with a hellish voice and a rattle in his hand, he sprinkled a circle of meal about the fire and commenced his conjuration."*

After spending some time here he was taken to the court of Powhatan. Powhatan at this time ruled like a monarch. He had thirty tribes that were subject to his rule, but he ruled by consent of the governed. He is described as a strong powerfully built man of sixty, a noble figure.

Powhatan's capital was Werowocomoco. He is referred to as a king by the colonists. The description was as follows: *"Powhatan sat upon a raised seat before a fire, in a large house, clothed with a robe of raccoon skins, the tails hanging in ornamental array. He had a commanding presence natural in one born to rule with undisputed authority."* A young girl sat on each side of the king and around the room were warriors and women. They greeted Smith with a shout.

Smith's narrative states, *"the queen of Oppamatuck brought me water to wash,"* and he was magnificently entertained as a distinguished guest of the king. Then his tale goes on. *"A long consultation*

was held, but the conclusion was, two great stones were brought be-
fore Powhatan. Then as many as could, laid hands on me, dragged
me to them, and thereon laid down my head, and being ready with
their clubs to beat out my brains. But, Pocohontas, the king's dear-
est daughter, when no entreaty could prevail, got my head in her
arms, and laid her own upon mine to save me from death; whereat
the emperor was contented, I should live to make him hatchets and
her bells, beads and copper, for they thought me as knowledgeable of
all occupations as themselves."

Powhatan kept Smith for two more days and then told him he
could return to the colony, instructing him to send him as gifts two
cannons and a grindstone, as he wanted to put his tribe on equal foot-
ing armament-wise as the colonists. He supplied Smith with guides
for the return trip, and Smith, after a demonstration of the cannon,
offered two of them to the Indians. But they found them too heavy
and settled for less cumbersome gifts.

During that winter, Smith again visited Powhatan and he was received well at this time. He brought Captain Newport along. Captain
Newport at first refused to go ashore, imagining that the foot bridges
built by Powhatan's tribe were traps. But after seeing Smith's journey into the Indian camp, Captain Newport came also and brought
along items that he felt the Indians would barter corn for. He met
limited success. Then he tried to trade directly with Powhatan. Powhatan informed him that it was beneath his dignity to trade in this
bickering manner. He told the Captain, *"Just put in front of me*
what you have to barter and I will give you corn of equal value."
But Powhatan's sense of this corn's value was higher than what the
Captain thought.

Later John Smith traded some beads that he called chief's beads
and got a very high price in corn.

King James of England decided that since Powhatan was a native
king he should be crowned and so he sent a crown, scarlet cloak and
many other presents, including a bed and furniture set. Captain
Smith and Newport were to do the honors. So they set out for Powhatan's village. They had a hard time getting him to kneel. Finally
one man leaned on him to get him to stoop a little and with the help
of three others, they crowned him. Then they fired their muskets in
salute. This startled Powhatan and, for a moment, he felt he was
about to be attacked. But then he saw all was well.

After this, for a period of time, Powhatan cautioned his tribes in regard to dealings with white men. He felt that they were increasing in strength too much, and that they were also cheating the natives. However, Captain Smith made another visit in the winter of 1608.

He took along 46 men and a small ship with two barges. Captain Smith said when he arrived that he wished to trade. Powhatan, realizing the need to protect his people from the strength of the British offered to trade corn only for guns and swords. But Captain Smith told him he would either trade for beads and copper or they would use force to take the corn from the Indians. Powhatan replied, *"I will spare you what I can, and that within two days. But, Captain, I am informed that you wish to conquer more than to trade, and at all events you know my people must be afraid to come near you with their corn, so long as you go armed and with such a retinue. Lay aside your weapons then. Here they are needless. We are all friends, all Powhatans."*

But Captain Smith would not do this. After some dispute they completed the trade, not to the Indians' satisfaction, though, as the threats of force were used. At high water Smith sailed away leaving three Germans to help the Indian king construct a white man type house.

From then on there was constant distrust between Powhatan's people and the English colonists. The white men were afraid that the Indians would become angry over their land expansion and would either go to war or refuse to deliver any more corn. And all this time Smith's people were still inquiring of a salt sea or ocean beyond, believing that there were tribes living there that had gold. They still wanted to get rich quick and go back to England.

After Captain John Smith returned to England, Powhatan's people became more hostile toward the colonists, and if it hadn't been for the efforts of Pocohontas, they might have run the colonists out of the country.

Six months after the departure of Smith from the colony, the population of whites had dropped from 600 to sixty people. They were living on nuts and roots and berries and had even become cannibals, digging up a dead Indian they had slain for food. Another man killed his wife and had eaten part of her. This colonist was hanged for the crime.

In 1613, two ships came to Jamestown to reinforce the colonists there. Captain Argall, who commanded one of the ships, decided to kidnap Pocohontas who was visiting with a neighboring tribe. Promising that no harm would come to Pocohontas, Argall got the help of a chief and enticed Pocohontas aboard his ship. There, leaving her a prisoner of the English, the Captain now told Pocohontas that she must sail to Jamestown and there work out a peace agreement with her father.

The colonists now dispatched messengers to Powhatan and told him that he must return all English arms in his possession and all English captives in exchange for the release of Pocohontas, and that he must conclude a firm peace.

But Powhatan didn't respond immediately to the English. In 1617, the Jamestown Colony sent a force of 150 men out against Powhatan. They were well armed and had Pocohontas with them. The Powhatans responded that if the colonists wanted to fight, they would accommodate them.

The colonists rushed the camp and destroyed the Indian village. They proceeded up the river and made a truce at the next village, and these people sent a message to Powhatan. Powhatan sent two of his brothers to inquire of Pocohontas' health, and they were happy to see she was all right.

During Pocohontas' stay at Jamestown, a young man named John Rolfe proposed marriage to her. When she accepted, and when Powhatan was contacted, he responded happily to this offer and from then to the time of his death gave support and tried to get along with the colonists the best he could.

Pocohontas went to England at a later date and there she died. Apparently the breathing of the London fog was too much for her.

Powhatan was a well built man and was still able to do a good day's work in his garden even though he was around 60 years old when he came in contact with the colonists. He had fine intelligence and was able to rule and command the respect of some thirty tribes.

My regret is that in research the only sources available are the accounts of John Smith and a little information from one or two other historians. However, at this time, they all regarded the Indians as savages and felt the English had a right to dispossess them from their lands in any way they wished.

Chapter 16

CRAZY HORSE

In watching the panorama of history you notice that often it is one outstanding incident that brings a man to everlasting fame and prominence. Crazy Horse might have passed by the white historian's eye unnoticed but for the Battle of the Little Big Horn, often referred to by white historians as the Custer massacre. But, as my friend Dallas Chief Eagle says, *"Smile. We won that one."*

Crazy Horse was born the son of a Sioux holy man. His father was also known as Crazy Horse, but after the son had his vision in which lightning and a spirited horse were shown to him, and when he proved himself as a warrior, he also was given the name Crazy Horse. He was very light complected, having light brown curly hair and very fair-skinned features. When he was a boy the Indians called him Curley. Whenever early whites saw him they thought he was a white captive who had been raised by the Lakota, or Sioux, as history most often calls his tribe.

Crazy Horse was always a very quiet man, but when something had to be done, he was there doing it. He was a respected leader of his people. While yet a young man he became a shirt wearer -- one of the young chiefs who had great responsibility to protect the tribe and keep peace in it. He was dead set against liquor and he saw what the white man's poison did -- how it caused an Indian to do violence against his own people. He saw buffalo robes sold for a jug of whiskey, and that not even good whiskey, for the traders would put in half water and then mix in red pepper and tobacco to give it fire.

Crazy Horse spent much time fasting and alone in the hills searching for ways to help his people.

When Crazy Horse was young, his band lived down by Fort Laramie along what the Sioux called the Holy Road. This was the Immigrant Trail and the Sioux had made a solemn treaty that they would not touch these people on this trail. So then it was called the Holy Road. But an incident occured which drove the Indians north.

A group of Mormon immigrants coming west had a cow run away. The owner chased it, but when it ran to the Indian encampment he became frightened and reported it to the commander at the fort as stolen. In the meantime, a visiting Indian from a northern Sioux band shot the cow.

The commander dispatched soldiers under an arrogant young Lieutenant Grattan who had very little use or understanding for the Indians. He was very concerned about property -- that is, white man's property, -- but no regard for justice or law according to the Indians. He came out to Conquering Bear, the friendly chief of the tribe. He insisted that they surrender the man who had killed the cow. The chief refused and said he couldn't because the man was a guest from another band. Conquering Bear offered the Lieutenant five good horses in payment for the cow, much more than the cow was worth. But Lieutenant Grattan was not satisfied. He wanted the man to be surrendered.

Chief Conquering Bear finally turned to try and talk the young man into surrendering. But the impatient Lieutenant evidently misinterpreted this action and ordered his men to fire. Conquering Bear's brother was hit and fell wounded. Conquering Bear still tried to prevent further bloodshed, telling his people not to shoot at the soldiers. But Conquering Bear too was shot.

Now the fighting was in earnest. The Indians wiped out the soldiers and then fled north. So young Crazy Horse saw his first battle, not as a warrior, but as a young boy.

He saw that the white man had caused the start of the trouble, and now his people were going north to get away for the soldiers and more trouble. Crazy Horse saw the slaughter of Brule Sioux at Blue Water Creek, where white soldiers came in and fired on friendly Indians camped under an American flag. He came onto the battle scene soon afterward and saw where many women and children had been brutally killed by these beasts who claimed to be civilized. He saw how the soldiers treated the women who lived in what the Sioux called the women's camp next to the fort. He saw that it was the custom to get drunk and beat their women among these people.

Constantly people were coming in, returning to live with the northern tribes, and they told of starvation among the so-called friendlies who had come into the reservations or agencies. They told of how the soldiers would go out and kill old men and boys whom they found hunting rabbits and small game near the forts, and then they would boast to new recruits at the fort of how they scalped this wild Indian out in the hills. And who would do anything for the Indians among these people?

Crazy Horse was with the Red Cloud warriors when Fetterman rode out foolishly with eighty men. It was Crazy Horse who led the decoys so that Fetterman pursued twenty Indians in what he thought would be an easy victory. But when he got over the ridge, instead, his whole troop was wiped out. The whites called it a massacre, but the truth was, it was a decisive defeat for the white cavalry troops.

When Crazy Horse's young brother went on a hunting trip and was murdered by white miners, Crazy Horse went out alone, and camped for more than a month. He killed every white man who ventured out from the mining camps, where they had come illegally into Indian territory. Even those he shot with a gun, he drove a Sioux arrow into. They thought a whole war party was in the area. But as Crazy Horse's medicine told him, he never took any scalps.

The Oglalas, his band of Sioux, called him a strange man. He never spoke of or boasted of his deeds. When his friends were killed in battle, he would not mourn as others did, but would go out into the hills by himself. There the warriors would find him. He would tell them where there was meat to hunt or where enemies were at.

Crazy Horse loved a woman called Black Buffalo Woman. He courted her as a girl, but while away on a war party, she was given to another man who had more influence in her band, and also had more horses to offer. Later in life this woman decided to leave her husband and come to Crazy Horse. This was done openly, and a Dakota woman had this right. So Crazy Horse took her along on a hunt.

But her former husband became angry at this Indian divorce -- not that he loved her so much, but because she came from an important family and he wanted to keep her for this influence. So he went after

Crazy Horse and tried to kill him. Though badly wounded, Crazy Horse survived. Black Buffalo Woman returned to her people and later gave birth to a daughter by Crazy Horse.

Crazy Horse remained without a woman for some time. He was a great man, yet always very poor. He kept only a few horses for hunting and war. The rest he always gave away. Whenever he went on a hunt, the women who had no husbands and the old people were the first to get food. Always the first thought in his mind was, how can I best help my people? Of all of history's Indian leaders, this was truly the most selfless one. Here was a man who could have worn a headdress that dragged on the ground. But always there was only one feather in his hair, his waist-length braids wrapped with otter fur and his red hawk medicine that was part of his vision. Beyond that, nothing.

When his friends asked him, *"Why not a bonnet?"* he would put a little grass in his hair and say, *"Oh they know I'm Crazy Horse anyway."*

The Crow and other tribes were always afraid of Crazy Horse. They said, *"He has strange powers. He rides through our bullets and arrows and they fall off him like rain."*

His band decided that it was not good for Crazy Horse to live alone without a wife, so they prevailed upon another woman to come and be a wife to this strange warrior chief. Crazy Horse accepted her, and in time learned to love her very much. He had a daughter by her, and this little girl was a real joy to him. He enjoyed playing with her. But she caught the white man's coughing sickness, TB, and when she died from it, Crazy Horse was wild with grief. Here was another fever from the hated white man and this thing called civilization.

Crazy Horse again went on the warpath by himself and killed white men who had brought this sickness into the Indian country. Crazy Horse watched Colonel Custer and his men as they went into the sacred Black Hills. These were lands that were held sacred to the Sioux. But Custer had gone to the Black Hills without permission from the Indians. His men and government had no respect for the treaty promises made to the Sioux, and soon his men had come back telling that there was gold in the hills.

Now there was no turning back of the white man. His greed was aroused. The miners followed the trail that Custer blazed. The Sioux killed many, but more kept coming. The trail across Sioux country was there. And besides this, the white man was systematically killing off the buffalo. Where once there were great herds of these wonderful creatures, now there were only a few scattered animals. The hide hunters had slaughtered them and left only their carcasses to rot, -- yet another reason to hate the white man.

Red Cloud and Spotted Tail, great Sioux chiefs, had come in to the reservation with their followers. The government had set up agencies. Now they were on reservations, waiting for rations that never came. And now the government had let it be known that all Indians who remained out from the agency would be regarded as hostiles. They must come in and surrender at the forts. This order was given in the winter of 1875 -- 1876. The weather was so bad that even the messengers had a hard time getting through. Yet whole villages must come in to starve at the white man's forts, or else they would be hunted as hostiles. And this was happening in the Sioux's own country.

Troops were being sent against them for no other reason than their desire to live upon the land that the Great Spirit had given them. And so, in the dead of winter, armies were sent out to destroy the Indian villages with their food supplies, and kill or capture the people. (If I weren't a hostile, with that kind of treatment, I'd be one soon!) Who would like to have someone come into his little town in the middle of the winter and burn down his home and round up his family and put them in a concentration camp? That is what the United States government did to the American Indian. *[Author's note: Because of this behavior by the white man, there was a saying among the hostiles: "If you have only one arrow and are between a rattlesnake and a white man, kill the white man. The rattlesnake will not strike if you do not bother him. But never trust a white man, especially around your land or women."]*

Then in March, General George Crook left the North Platte River with ten companies of cavalry and two of infantry. Two Moons, a northern Cheyenne chief, had decided with his people to surrender. They were camped on the Little Powder River. But Crook's scouts found them and brought up the cavalry, and on March 17, 1876, Colonel J.J. Reynolds attacked them with six companies of cavalry. They charged the camp, taking it by surprise. They shot into the tipis, killing men, women and children. The Indians fled up a hill, and as soon as the warriors could regroup, they counter-attacked. Driving the cavalry back, they held them there until the women and children could escape to Crazy Horse's camp.

Colonel Reynolds burned the Indian camp and retreated to where Crook was camped. The troopers were almost without supplies and so General Crook and his men returned to the Platte River. Two Moons and his people were now with Crazy Horse and would fight along with them.

The Oglalas made Crazy Horse their head chief, and messengers were sent to recruit other Indians to fight, including some from Spotted Tail and Red Cloud agencies. Now various groups moved to the Rosebud Creek area in Montana. There were still buffalo to hunt there. Many Sioux and Cheyenne from other bands now joined them.

In June, the Hunkpapa Sioux had their sun dance. Sitting Bull, the medicine man, cut fifty little pieces of skin from each of his arms and then gave the sun dance, staring at the sun and dancing until he fell in a faint as if dead. Now he told his vision; *"Many soldiers come. They will be like grasshoppers with their heads pointed down. They will fall dead into our camp."*

General Crook was coming with 1300 troops. He had Crow Indian scouts, but the Sioux were ready for him this time. Crazy Horse was out hunting him with better than a thousand warriors, and these were warriors not just bent on coups, but knowing that the only way to turn back the soldiers was to defeat them. Their cry was, *"Remember the helpless ones and fight hard. It's a good day to die!"*

On the morning of June 17, Crazy Horse's warriors found the cavalry. They made first contact with the Crow scouts. The Crows rode back to warn the cavalry, but by this time, the Sioux were upon them.

Crazy Horse was everywhere. He was the man of his vision. He had white hailstone spots on his cheeks and behind his ear a small polished stone. Part of Crook's command under Captain Guy V. Henry was cut off. Captain Henry was shot in the head and left by his own retreating men. But the Crow and Shoshone scouts charged back and forced their way through the Sioux warriors. They rescued Captain Henry. There were other brave deeds.

A Cheyenne woman saw her brother's horse shot out from under him. Quick as a flash she rode out to rescue him. He leaped behind her and rode to safety.

This was a time of brave deeds, and the Indians fought hard. Crazy Horse lost eleven good warriors and some more were wounded, while Crook had 57 killed and wounded and there were 34 killed and wounded among the scouts. Crook, his supplies exhausted, fell back to his base on Goose Creek, near the present site of Sheridan, Wyoming.

Crazy Horse moved to the valley of the Little Big Horn. Here was the main Sioux and Cheyenne encampment. The Sioux felt that they were safe for a time. After all, Crook had left the country.

But now the scouts had reported new cavalry coming. This time it was the long hair Custer with six hundred troops plus Indian scouts. Four brave Cheyenne rode out to meet Custer's men.

Custer had split his command. Major Marcus Reno and three companies were ordered to move straight to the Little Big Horn and cross the river and attack the southern end of the Indian village. Custer took five companies with him and he was going to attack the northern end of the camp. Captain Benteen would hold three companies in reserve to use as reinforcements.

Custer was still concerned about the Indians escaping. He didn't believe his scouts who had said, *"Too many Sioux. Stay away."* Custer saw the Sioux women and children moving back and he shouted to his men, *"Hurry up or there won't be enough Indians to kill!"*

Meanwhile, Major Reno had engaged the Sioux at the southern end of their village. Crazy Horse charged them, leading Oglalas and men under Crow King and Gall. His cry was, *"Be brave, Lakotas. It's a good day to die!"*

Major Reno tried to form a skirmish line and dismounted his men. But the Sioux cut them to ribbons. Reno finally led them in retreat to a ridge where they took up defense positions, and where he was reinforced by Benteen's men. But now most of the Sioux had turned their attention to a new threat. Custer's five companies were attacking from the north end. Custer, seeing the size of the village, now dispatched a rider to Benteen. *"Bring packs. Come quick,"* it said. He knew he would need more ammunition.

Custer never made it to the village. The Indians hit him as he started to ford the river. The Indians kept pushing him back. Now he was surrounded on all sides. Chief Gall, leading the Hunkpapas, and Crazy Horse with the Oglalas struck like two hurricanes! Crazy Horse led his men straight at the soldiers, and the Cheyenne who were there remembered that this was *"squaw-killer Custer."* These were not coup-seeking warriors. They didn't stop in the middle of the battle to merely touch a dead soldier or grab up plunder. These men wanted only one thing – the death of every murderer that followed yellow-haired Custer.

Custer had boasted that given him the Seventh Cavalry, *"he'd ride through the whole Sioux nation."* Now his five companies were almost annihilated, and those who remained formed a circle for a defensive position. But now the Sioux who swarmed over them literally chopped them to pieces. In a little more than an hour after the fight began, Custer's command was no more.

As the Sioux went over the bodies of Custer's men, they found many had flasks of whiskey on them. Some of the soldiers shot themselves to keep from being captured. Now the Sioux renewed the attack on Major Reno's men, but they were dug in between rocks on top of a hill, so the Indians broke off the engagement.

The next morning, they started up the fight again, but their scouts reported more troops coming, these under General Terry and Gibbon. So the great Sioux encampment broke up, Sitting Bull taking his people and going to Canada, and the other bands going to their hunting grounds.

When General Terry arrived, he ordered Major Reno to assemble his troops. *"They're here, sir,"* Major Reno replied. All he had left of combat-ready men were some sixty men. Yet a year later the army held a court-martial inquiry as to why he didn't go to the rescue of Custer against 3000 Sioux. The military wanted a scapegoat for Custer's folly.

But Crazy Horse knew that the white man wouldn't rest until the last Indian was put on a reservation. General Crook and Terry were both searching for Indians. Iron Plume, on September 9, was attacked by Crook's men. He sent word for Crazy Horse to come and help him, but Crazy Horse arrived too late. Iron Plume had already been forced to surrender. Other bands were being forced to come into the agencies.

Red Cloud and Spotted Tail, the agency chiefs, were now competing with each other, and through them scouts were sent to Crazy

Horse's camp. General Miles was trying to get Crazy Horse to surrender to him. Everyone wanted some of the glory of getting the surrender of this last great hostile chief. Crazy Horse sent in nine men from his people under a flag of truce. He wanted to talk to Miles in regard to peace. But as his men approached the fort they were fired on by scalp-hungry Crow scouts who killed five of these peace men. The rest returned to Crazy Horse.

Crazy Horse was determined to stay out. But more peace messengers came from the agencies.

In January, General Miles led his troops out against Crazy Horse. The troops were dressed in heavy buffalo coats. They found and followed Crazy Horse's trail. The Indians fought the best they could, but soon they were down to hand to hand combat, as there was no ammunition left. While the warriors held back the soldiers, the women and children escaped.

Now more peace men came and even Spotted Tail himself. They brought much food and many gifts.

In May, General Crook told Crazy Horse that if he would come into Red Cloud agency, that he would accept his surrender there and then make arrangements for an agency of his own. So, on May 5, 1877, the last great hostile came in. They marched in behind their brave leader. Here came Crazy Horse and his war chief, and then the warriors, all still proudly carrying their war shields, guns and lances. As they neared the fort, they broke out in war songs, a proud, beautiful sight, yet sad, for here came in the last of the free Plains Indians.

When they came in, Crook made them surrender their guns and horses. After Crazy Horse came into the agency, some of the agency Indians became jealous. Here was the great hostile chief and still his young men followed him around. No Water, who hated Crazy Horse from the wife incident, now had his friends spreading rumors that Crazy Horse would go on the warpath again. When an army officer asked if Crazy Horse would go with his men to fight the Nez Perce Indians, he refused at first. Then he said he would go and fight until not a Nez Perce was left. The interpreter, who belonged to the anti-Crazy Horse group, translated it, *"I will go and fight until not a white man is left."* The officers refused to believe a correct translation, and so they reported to General Crook.

The General decided to talk to Crazy Horse himself, but he was

met by No Water's friends who told him that Crazy Horse had said
he would kill him. Crook believed the man and called in all the agency chiefs. They were all petty little men afraid of the power of the
great Oglala, and advised the General to kill him. But Crook ordered
out men to arrest him.

Crazy Horse decided to go to the Spotted Tail agency, hoping to be
heard there. Crazy Horse went to talk to the army commander at the
agency. He explained that he wanted to move to the Spotted Tail
agency because at the other agency there was only trouble for him.
Major Lee listened, but he said he must go back to Fort Robinson.
Major Lee said he would try to square things for Crazy Horse at Fort
Robinson and he rode back with him. But when Crazy Horse arrived
back at that agency, they told him he must go directly to the fort,
and when he got there, he was taken directly to the guard house.

Now the man who'd ridden free all his life saw the bars where the
white man would imprison him. He knew that there would be no one
to talk for him. He pulled a knife from under his blanket. But an
Indian tried to hold back his arms and the guard drove a bayonnet
into his back and drew it out, only to drive it in again. Crazy Horse
said, *"Let me go, my friends. You have hurt me enough already."*
They laid him on the floor.

Now the whole Sioux encampment knew the great war chief was
dying and everyone was ashamed, for their own people had a hand in
it. And now Crazy Horse's father came to sit by him, and Touch-The-
Clouds, his tall cousin. Then Crazy Horse spoke his last words.

*"My father, I am badly hurt. Tell the people it is no use to depend
on me any more now."* And with that, one of the bravest, most un-
selfish leaders the American Indian had known died.

Chapter 17

SOME CHIEFS OF THE EAST AND MIDWEST

MASSASOIT, A SACHEM OF THE WAMPANOAG

Massasoit was the first Indian chief or sachem known to the Plymouth colony. He was introduced to the Plymouth colony by Samoset and Squanto. Squanto had previously been a slave who was captured by an early sailing vessel that had visited that shore.

Massasoit came to visit Plymouth colony with sixty men. Squanto explained that they were friendly and wished peace. An agreement of peace was made, and Massasoit gave the Plymouth colony a large tract of land. This was land upon which the former inhabitants had died of some pestilence.

The Indians established trade with the colony, trading them furs and also seed corn.

Massasoit lived with the colonists for 50 years, and yet maintained peace. The surrounding chiefs who gave him allegiance spoke always of his kindness to them, and while he was a great chief, having many settlements under him, yet he never possessed any wealth himself. His only adornment that distinguished him from others was a bone bead necklace.

KING PHILIP OR METACOM

King Philip was the youngest son of Massasoit. He became chief after the death of his older brother, Alexander, who died at the hands of the Plymouth colonists. In spite of this, Philip went in and pledged himself to the peace that his father had made with the Plymouth colony.

But then in 1671, the English started trespassing on his hunting grounds. Continual disregard for the rights of Indians, and encroachment upon their lands resulted in war. This war in history is known as the King Philip War. King Philip, through his efforts and energy, was able to induce many other tribes to join in battle with his own people against the colonies. King Philip had a force of 600 men of his own, and the powerful Narragansetts, Nipmucks, the Indians of Connecticut, and those of Maine also joined him.

The King Philip War was fought in 1675 and 1676. He was all over the frontier, exhorting and encouraging tribes to fight for the Indian race as a whole. He showed great courage and skill at all times. But his loss to the English was due to superior arms and the enemy having more manpower.

In all his warfare, Philip never mistreated any captives. Yet the English were torturing and hanging his people and even selling them as slaves abroad.

King Philip was finally cornered in a swamp and shot by soldiers under a military man named Church. After his death, rather than giving him a decent burial, the barbaric English had him quartered and his head was carried to Plymouth colony, there to be displayed at their Thanksgiving.

Philip's only son, a boy of nine, was sold into slavery by these same people.

BLACK HAWK

Black Hawk belonged to the Sauk tribe of Indians. He was a man of keen intelligence, a brave warrior, and had strong love of his people. Black Hawk is remembered in history for the Black Hawk War that was forced onto him in 1832.

His village was located where Rock Island, Illinois stands and was called Saukenuk. Here was the home of Black Hawk & Sauk and Fox.

The Fox were originally a separate tribe, but they now spoke the same language and lived together. Their first trouble with white men came in 1804 when the Americans invited some Sauk and Fox chiefs to St. Louis, got them drunk and induced them to put their marks on a treaty selling all of their tribal grounds east of the Mississippi to the Americans and some of their land **west** of the Mississippi. This was one of the rottenest deals ever pulled by the United States, paying only $2,234.50 to the chiefs and promising them an annual payment in goods of $600 to the Sauk tribe and $400 to the Fox. The Indians who went to St. Louis had no right or authority to sell any land, and they thought all the United States wanted to secure was permission to hunt on these lands -- not buy them.

During the war of 1812, Black Hawk's warriors fought on the side of the British and sent 500 men to fight at Detroit under Tecumseh. They continued to be hostile to the Americans until the end of this war and even afterwards.

In 1828, white settlers moved in and started taking over the Indian lands, even dividing up their fields and possessions. This was done while Black Hawk's band was away on a hunt. This and other action finally forced Black Hawk on the warpath, and in 1832, 1500 volunteer militia men marched against him. A Major Isaiah Stillman commanded 275 of these brave souls. These men, finding that Black Hawk was only 25 miles distant, asked permission to go ahead of the main troops and attack.

Black Hawk had been trying to get help from the Potawatomis, and having failed in this, was thinking of surrendering in order to avoid bloodshed. Hearing that the troops were approaching, he sent three men under a white flag to talk to them, and five men to stay at a distance and see what the result would be. When the three Indians arrived at the militia men's camp, the soldiers became excited, and spotting the other five Indians in the distance, gave pursuit of them. They killed two of the five and the other three returned to warn Black Hawk. Then the soldiers pursued the Indians. But Black Hawk prepared an ambush with the forty warriors he had with him. They opened fire, shooting several of the band of volunteers. Seeing now that it wasn't going to be a matter of just shooting at defenseless, unaware Indians, the military volunteers beat a hasty retreat. Black Hawk sent 25 warriors on their trail to speed them up.

When they got back to Stillman's camp they told that there were thousands of wild Indians in pursuit, and this so unnerved the cavalrymen that the whole brave command went running back to General Whitesides. This bunch of military volunteers had had enough Indian fighting, and so they raised 2000 more men to send against Black Hawk and his poor people.

Meanwhile, Black Hawk's people were struggling for survival and trying to move back to join up with their own people. They realized that resistance was useless, and only wanted to cross the Mississippi River where they hoped to find safety in the land that still belonged to them. But another force was in field under a Colonel Dodge. His men attacked the Indians, but Black Hawk and fifty of his braves drove off the troops.

After this, some of Black Hawk's people decided to separate off from him and try to go down the Wisconsin River and cross the Mississippi. But many of these were killed by soldiers. Now General Atkinson had taken the trail in pursuit of Black Hawk's band. They caught up to them, and what few warriors were left fought back the best they could. But they were no match for 1300 troops. The Americans shot and clubbed men, women and children while many of the Indians tried to escape by swimming the river. But these were also shot and the Americans had brought up a gunboat with a six-pound cannon on it. This was also used against the Indians.

After eight hours the Indian dead were counted -- 150 bodies plus many more who had been shot and drowned in the river -- something of great pride to a country whose military commanders are always happy for large body counts. There were 30 prisoners taken, all women and children. Truly a great victory for the United States government!

Black Hawk, the 65 year old chief who led this band, now went to the Winnebago and asked them to go with him that he might surrender with the few people he had left.

"You have taken me prisoner with all my warriors," **Black Hawk** said. *"I am much grieved, for I expected, if I did not defeat you, to hold out much longer and give you more trouble before I surrendered. I tried hard to bring you into ambush, but your last general understands Indian fighting. The first one was not so wise. When I saw that I could not beat you by Indian fighting, I determined to rush on you and fight you face to face. I fought hard. But your guns were well aimed. The bullets flew like birds in the air, and whizzed by our ears like the wind through the trees in winter. My warriors fell around me; it began to look dismal. I saw my evil day at hand. The sun rose dim on us in the morning, and at night it sunk in a dark cloud, and looked like a ball of fire. That was the last sun that shone*

on Black Hawk. His heart is dead and no longer beats quick in his bosom. He is now a prisoner to the white man; they will do with him as they wish. But he can stand torture, and is not afraid of death. He is no coward. Black Hawk is an Indian.

He has done nothing for which an Indian has been ashamed. He has fought for his countrymen, the squaws, and papooses, against white men, who came year after year to cheat him and take away their lands. You know the cause of our making war. It is known to all white men. They ought to be ashamed of it. The white men despise the Indians and drive them from their homes. But the Indians are not deceitful. The white men speak bad of the Indian and look at him spitefully. But the Indian tells the truth. Indians do not steal.

Black Hawk is a true Indian and disdains to cry like a woman. He feels for his wife, his children, and friends. But he does not care for himself. He cares for his nation and other Indians. They will suffer. He laments their fate. The white men do not scalp the head; but they do worse, they poison the heart; it is not pure with them. His country men will not be scalped, but they will, in a few years, become like the white men, so that you can't trust them, and there must be, as in the white settlements, nearly as many officers as men, to take care of them and keep them in order.

Farewell, my nation: Black Hawk tried to save you and avenge your wrongs. He drank the blood of some of the whites. He has been taken prisoner, and his plans are stopped. He can do no more. He is near his end. His sun is setting, and he will rise no more. Farewell to Black Hawk."

After his surrender, he was sent to prison at Fort Monroe, and during his time back east he was taken before the President of the United States. At that time he spoke these words; "You are a man, and I am another. Do with me as you will. I know that you will give me fair treatment. We did not expect to conquer the whites. No, they had too many horses, too many men. I took up the hatchet for my part, to revenge the injuries which my people could no longer endure. Had I borne them longer without striking, my people would have said, 'Black Hawk is a woman. He is too old to be a chief. He is no Sauk'. These reflections caused me to raise the war whoop. I say no more of it; it is known to you. Keokuk once was here; you took him by the hand, and when he wished to return to his home you were willing. Black Hawk expects that like Keokuk, we shall be permitted to return too."

Black Hawk was allowed to go to the Sauk and Fox reservation where he died October 3, 1838. The white man paid him one more act of disgrace. His grave was dug up and the bones taken.

Wolf Robe, the Southern Cheyenne who joined with Dull Knife. Courtesy *Bureau of American Ethnology.*

Chapter 18

INDIAN LEADERSHIP

TECUMSEH

Tecumseh was born to the Shawnee tribe in Ohio in 1768. His name meant Shooting Star. He saw the encroachment and westward movement of the Americans after the Revolutionary War.

Tecumseh tried to unite all the tribes against the white man's expansion. He went from tribe to tribe contacting the Creeks in the south, and the Sioux and Chippewa in distant Minnesota clear to the Canadian border.

For a time, he and his brother worked together. His brother was called Tenskwatawa, the Open Door. He was referred to by the whites as the Prophet, and when they established an Indian town at Tippecanoe River in Indiana, it was called Prophet Town.

Tecumseh proclaimed that all the land under Indians belonged to all the Indians and could not be sold by individual tribes or chiefs. He showed himself to be not only a great warrior, but also an orator and organizer. He forbade liquor among his people.

Tecumseh was once in love with a beautiful white girl, and she wanted to marry him, but she told him he must give up his Indian ways, and he realized he could never do this.

William Henry Harrison, governor of Indiana Territory was always pushing for more lands for the white settlers, and when he came to talk to Tecumseh, they sat on a bench. Tecumseh started pushing Governor Harrison over and kept this up until he was about to be pushed off the bench. When the governor complained, Tecumseh said, *"See? That's what you are doing to the Indians -- pushing them always out of the land."*

Tataⁿka Yotaⁿka or Sitting Buffalo Bull.   Best known as Sitting Bull.
1834-1890. Medicine man and warrior.

Bureau of American Ethnology Collection

In 1811, while Tecumseh was south on a trip recruiting other tribes to his cause, William Henry Harrison attacked the Prophet Town. The Indians fought back, but being in small numbers, they were forced to abandon their town. Tecumseh was very angry with his brother for allowing the Indians to be drawn into battle before the time he had set.

Now there was raiding by other tribes along the frontier, but not the united effort. The following year, 1812, Tecumseh joined the British. He had an army that varied between 1000 and 3000 warriors.

In the War of 1812, it was Tecumseh's warriors who were the deciding factor in the capture of Detroit. All during this war, Tecumseh showed himself an able general and a brave warrior. One of the British commanders, General Proctor, allowed the Indians who were fighting with him to kill and torture prisoners. When one of Tecumseh's men told him of this, he immediately came storming over to the camp, and, knocking down the Indians who were doing it, he called them cowardly for torturing and killing defenseless men and told the British commander he was not fit to command.

Now a larger force was marching against the British. General Proctor was in retreat and Tecumseh wanted him to stand and fight. General Harrison was coming with a force of 3500 troops while the British had 700 men and Tecumseh's 1000 Indians. With the first attack the British general fled. The British troops surrendered. But Tecumseh ordered his Indians to fight on. Even though wounded many times, he continued to fight. But when darkness came upon the battlefield, a bullet struck and killed Tecumseh. However, his men would not leave his body to be found. It was taken away and buried. Thus ended the life of a great Shawnee.

THE LEADERS

Yes, these were all brave men who fought and worked for their people, and there were many more.

There was Sitting Bull, the Hunkpapa medicine man who was murdered in 1891, and Little Crow, who led the Sioux uprising of 1864 in Minnesota and took his people on the warpath. He was the one who asked the agent for food because his people were starving, and the agent told them to eat grass. It was this treatment that drove Little Crow on the warpath.

John Ross, Cherokee leader who witnessed the tragedy of the Trail of Tears.

Courtesy *Bureau of American Ethnology.*

Captain Jack, a leader in the Modoc War of 1872-73. Hanged at Fort Klamath, October 3, 1873.

Courtesy *Bureau of American Ethnology.*

There was Nana, the eighty-year-old Apache who went on a 600 mile war-trail, fighting off Texas Rangers and cavalry. Victorio was another brave Apache leader who fought back for his land.

Captain Jack, the Modoc led his men into the lava beds of northern California and there they made such a brave stand that it took 1500 soldiers to drive them out.

And what of Dull Knife and Wolf Robe who led their Cheyennes across hundreds of miles, fighting off myriads of troops? This was their journey from Oklahoma to try to return to their home country in southern Montana.

Roman Nose, another Cheyenne chief, fought bravely for his people, and to drive off buffalo hunters that came to slaughter the buffalo for the hides. He died at the Beecher Island fight.

There was John Ross, the Cherokee who worked to save his people from removal to the Indian Territory, and then worked to protect them while they were being removed on what is now called the Trail of Tears. Eighteen thousand people marched out from lands that they held by solemn treaty and every other right. But the white man found gold in the North Carolina and Tennessee hills, so the Indians had to be removed.

Sequoyah, the greatest of the Cherokee developed an alphabet for his people that they might learn to read and write.

Chief Seattle preached peace with the whites, but still tried his best to save his peoples land. The city of Seattle, Washington is named after him.

And there was Plenty Coups, the chief of the Montana Crows whose achievements were so great that his bonnet and trailer extended and dragged clear on the ground. His tribe said that because he was so great a man, they would pay him the highest honor. They would have no chief after him.

There was Wovoka, the Paiute who founded the Ghost Dance religion, and Cornplanter and Red Jacket. There was Handsome Lake, Hiawatha and others. These are our heros. They gave our people greatness. They showed courage when they were needed -- great and good men. Let them be remembered.

Little Crow, or the Hawk who Hunts Walking, Mdewakanton Sioux
Leader.   Courtesy *Bureau of American Ethnology.*

Dull Knife, the Northern Cheyenne who died in 1883.
                Courtesy *Bureau of American Ethnology.*

Chapter 19

INDIANS TODAY

Today the survivors of the once numerous tribes who populated the United States are, for the most part, on reservations. Reservations are lands that were set aside for the tribes by the government. This land was the part the early settlers didn't want. But even these worthless acres have been whittled down, and many of the reservations are gone completely. In Canada, the land kept aside for the Indians is called reserves.

The Navajos are the largest tribe today. Numbering 115,000, they have a reservation spread over four western states. They originally were known for their sheep raising and blankets, rugs, and silver smithing. But today the tribe operates a large saw mill, motels, gas leases, oil leases, and some of the tribe supplies cucumbers to a large pickle factory. They have an industrial park, and a large electronics firm that employs many Navajos.

The Sioux Indians are the second largest tribe, with a population of 60,000. They are principally in North and South Dakota and Montana. Today they raise cattle or secure work in surrounding towns. There is a great need for economic development on these and many other reservations.

The Chippewa Indians are the third largest tribe, with a population of 40,000. The Chippewas live in Michigan, Wisconsin, Minnesota, and North Dakota, and the non-treaty Chippewas live in Canada. These are the ones who refused to sign a treaty with the United States and moved to Canada instead. The Chippewa are well-known for their wild rice. They work also at logging and timber, and on one reservation we have a ball bearing factory. Some of us work as hunting and fishing guides, and do trapping in the winter, while others have gone to the major cities for work.

The White Mountain Apache in Arizona are cattle raisers. They have beautiful herds of Herefords. They also have a large saw mill industry, and recently began leasing home sites for summer homes in their mountain areas.

Several other tribes have tried to attract industries to their reservations. Efforts are being made to develop tourist and recreation attractions in reservation areas.

The Warm Springs, Oregon tribe has a hot springs resort.

The Cherokee tribe puts on a pageant called *"Unto These Hills."* It's put on at Cherokee, North Carolina each summer, and tells the story of their removal from their homes in Georgia and Tennessee to the Oklahoma Territory.

But there is much need for better living conditions. There is 40% unemployment on most Indian reservations. Many Indians only have seasonal work in the summer. The average Indian family's income is half that of the American Negro. The life expectancy to the average American is 65 to 70. The American Indians can expect to live to be 40 to 45.

A man who worked for a private agency studying health conditions and living problems came back from China, and said that conditions were worse on Indian reservations than they were in China. American Indians get less education than anyone in this country, and the Bureau of Indian Affairs Schools are of poorer quality than public schools. In the last few years there has been some effort toward higher education, but much more is needed. There is a need for a better approach to education in elementary and high school. These young people need to be motivated. There are some strong efforts that are encouraging. The University of New Mexico has a special school for Indian law students. This will give the tribes much needed Indian lawyers. Also, the United Scholarship Service fund in Denver, Colorado secures scholarships for Indian students.

Indian workers who have been trained and are working in industries located near or on Indian reservations have shown themselves to have an extremely high degree of reliability and steadiness on the job. The Indians have shown great adaptability to jobs that require dexterity and eye coordination. They appreciate the opportunity to work close to their homes. But before the current drive to bring jobs to the reservations, the Bureau of Indian Affairs had a program of relocation. Indians were sent to the major cities, and there were given jobs. But this program wasn't entirely successful. Many Indians had trouble adjusting to city living. Some became part of the skid row people in the cities. Indians ended up with their own ghetto areas -- Clark Street in Chicago, Bunker Hill in Los Angeles, and a certain section in Omaha, Nebraska. After having help landing their first job, the Indian relocation program is of no more help. Because of lacking job skills, they are at the bottom of the wage scale. Knowing little about the big city, they fall into money traps. They buy things on credit and then are unable to meet their payments. They lose their jobs and, unable to find other work, they might drift back to the reservation or end up on skid row.

But there are those who do make it. In the Los Angeles area alone there are 40,000 Indians. They have an Indian center, Indian churches, and an Indian basketball team.

In Los Angeles, you see a strong renaissance of Indian culture. There are several Indian pow wow and dance clubs; the Drum and Feather, Many Trails, Little Bighorn, Knife Chief Group, and American Indian Tribal Dancers. The Navajo have their own club called the Sand Painters. They have a day in September when they gather at Sycamore Grove. Almost every Saturday night there is a pow wow. Then each group has an annual pow wow which lasts all weekend long where everyone camps out. There you see campers and tipis. The dancers make their own costumes. These can cost into the hundreds of dollars, and you see little four and five year old children dancing along with the rest.

There are Indian centers in Seattle, San Francisco, Oakland, Tulsa, Phoenix, and Chicago. There are Indian dance groups in all these cities and in Detroit, New York, Houston, Dallas, Wichita, and Denver. Here in all these big cities Indians come together. They help their young people to learn and retain the old ways. They learn Indian dancing, the War Dance, the Scalp Dance, and 49er, the social dance. They learn how to make Indian stew and fry bread.

Indian art exhibits show painting done by modern artists in oil and water colors. There are arts and crafts representing the beadwork and buckskin craft of many tribes, pottery by Southwest Indians, the Hopi Kachinas, Navajo rugs and blankets, silver smithing by the Navajo, Hopi and Zuni craftsmen, baskets by Papago, Paiute and Hoopa, birchbark crafts by the Chippewa, totem pole carvings from Alaska. All are represented in these art shows. Yes, the Indian culture is yet alive and will come more alive.

What of reservation areas? Here's where we see the really big pow wows. The Crow Fair, on the Crow Reservation in Montana boasts of more tipis than any other Indian pow wow, and they have had as many as 400 tipis.

At All-American Indian Days at Sheridan, Wyoming, they hold the national Miss Indian America Contest, not only judged for beauty and poise, but most importantly, what the competing young women want to do in regard to their people, and what they are striving for in life. Each is judged on her knowledge of Indian affairs and Indian culture, and what she can do (Does she bead or did she make her own costume? Is her hair long without a wig? Does she paint or play any musical instrument?). The winner makes personal appearances all over the U.S., and also goes to travel through Europe.

The Gallup (New Mexico) Indian Ceremonials in early August is another big one with Indians coming from all over, including Mexico. Here they have Aztec and Totenac dancers, the Zuni Olla Maidens who walk with the pottery water jars on their heads, and lots of other groups. It is the biggest exhibit of Indian arts and crafts.

The Navajo Tribal Fair, run by the Navajo Tribe, is held in Flagstaff every 4th of July.

The pow wow trail extends back east clear to New York and Pennsylvania. At Tama, Iowa, there is a big Indian pow wow sponsored by the Sauk and Fox tribe. In the Oklahoma area there are pow wows all the time. So today the Indian people still remember their traditions and culture.

The American Indians have inspired many non-Indian groups -- the Boy Scouts, Woodcraft Rangers, High Y Clubs, and groups of older hobbyists. These people make a great study of Indian ways and crafts, not only in this country, but all over the world. Outside London, England, the English groups have an annual Indian pow wow. In Germany there is a park where Indian hobbyists shed their street clothes and become Indians.

Indian groups on tour have received great responses in Japan as well as in Europe.

We have Hollywood Indians. We have about 15 or 20 Indians who work in the motion picture or television industry. But Hollywood seems to think that white men should play Indians, so the Indians end up working as extras most of the time, playing the background. Hollywood has made a lot of money off the Indian people's history of suffering. But unfortunately, very little of this wealth has got to the Indians, and most of the stories are not done authentically. I know, because I worked there for ten years. I played cowboys and Indians, and only on rare occasions did they bother to get the true story. When they did, either myself or another man worked as technical director. But some of us still hope to see the day when Hollywood will tell more true stories.

Some of our young people have formed groups at colleges where they go to school, and they are speaking out on the needs of the Indians as they see them. There are real needs in this land of plenty. There is hunger on many reservations. There are needs for more and better housing. There are too many Indian families living in old car bodies and shacks. Of course there is a need for more industry and improved agriculture to provide more income and jobs on the reservations.

In writing this book, it is my hope to give the American people and friends of Indians in other lands a better understanding of my people, to let them know we still live and are not just in movies or museum exhibits, and perhaps through this, more people might understand our past and present. As my people say, Brothers, it is good to tell one's heart.

Sun Bear

SUGGESTED REFERENCES

Recommended List of Indian Books

At Home in the Wilderness. Sun Bear. Naturegraph Publishers.1968.

Beautyway: A Navajo Ceremonial. Haile, Bernard and Oakes, Maud Bollinger Series. 1957.

Black Elk Speaks. Neihardt, John. University of Nebraska Press. 1961.

Black Foot Lodge Tales. Grinnell, George Bird. University of Nebraska Press. 1962.

Book of the Hopi. Waters, Frank. The Viking Press. 1963.

Brave Warriors. Wiltsey, Norman. Caxton Printers. 1963.

Century of Dishonor, A. Jackson, Helen Hunt. Harper & Row, Publishers.

Cheyenne Autumn. Sandoz, Mari. Avon Books. 1964.

Comanches: Lords of the South Plains. Wallace, Ernest and Hoebel, Adamson E. University of Oklahoma Press. 1964.

Conspiracy of Pontiac. Parkman, Francis. Collier Press.

Crazy Horse. Sandoz, Mari. University of Nebraska Press. 1961.

Fighting Cheyennes, The. Grinnell, George Bird. University of Oklahoma Press. 1964.

Gospel of the Redman. Seton, Ernest T. Boy Scouts of America. 1963.

Great Upon The Mountain. Brown, Vinson. Naturegraph Publishers. 1970.

I Will Fight No More Forever. Beal, Merrill. University of Washington Press. 1963.

Indian, The: America's Unfinished Business. Brophy, William A. and Aberle, Sophie D. University of Oklahoma Press.

Indian Tales. De Angulo, Jaine. Hill & Wang, Inc. 1962.

Indians of America. Collier, John. New American Library. 1960.

Indiancraft. Hunt, Ben. Bruce Publishing Co.

Iroquois Book of Rites. Hale, Horatio; Editor. University of Toronto Press. 1963.

Ishi: In Two Worlds. Kroeber, Theodora. University of California Press. 1961.

Laughing Boy, *(A wonderful story of a Navajo youth).* La Farge, Oliver. Houghton Mufflin Co.

Long Death, The, *(The death of the Plains Tribes).* Andrist, Ralph K. The MacMillan Co. 1964.

Masked Gods, (Navajo & Pueblo Ceremonialism). Waters, Frank. Sage Books. 1962.

Modocs & Their War, The. Murray, Keith. University of Oklahoma Press. 1965.

Murder and Robbery of the Indians. Wagner, Earl. Candon Press. 1964.

Navajo Means People. Vogt, Evon Z. and Kluckhohn, Clyde. Harvard University Press. 1951.

Navajo Witchcraft. Kluckhohn, Clyde. Beacon Press. 1962.

Ojibwa Myths and Legends. Coleman, Bernard; Eich, Estelle; Frogner, Ellen; and Haines, Ross.

Our Brother's Keeper, *(The Indian in White America; an account of a great disgrace).* Cahn, Edgar S. New Community Press. 1969.

Pawnee Hero Stories and Folk Tales. Grinnell, George Bird. University of Nebraska Press. 1961.

Pictorial History of the American Indian, A. La Farge, Oliver. Crown Publishers. 1956.

Peyote Cult, The. La Barre, Weston. The Shoestring Press, Inc. 1964.

Plenty Coups: Chief of the Crows. Linderman, Frank B. University of Nebraska Press. 1962.

Quanah Parker. Jackson, Clyde and Grace. Exposition Press. 1963.

Red Antway of the Navajo. Wyman, Leland C. Museum of Navajo Ceremonial Art Press.

Red Cloud and the Sioux Problem. Olson, James C. University of Nebraska Press. 1965.

Red Cloud's Folk, *(A History of the Oglala Sioux Indians).* Hyde, George E. University of Oklahoma Press. 1957.

Saga of Chief Joseph. Howard, Helen Addison and Dan McGrath. Caxton Printers. 1965.

Seminoles, The. McReynolds, Edwin C. University of Oklahoma Press. 1957.

Shoshones, The, *(Sentinels of the Rockies).* Trenholm, Virginia Cole & Corley, Maurine. University of Oklahoma Press. 1964.

Sioux, The. Hassrich, Royal B. University of Oklahoma Press. 1964.

Sitting Bull. Vestal, Stanley. University of Oklahoma Press. 1965.

Southern Cheyenne, The. Berthrong, Donald J. University of Oklahoma Press. 1963.

Southern Indians, The. Cotterill, R. S. University of Oklahoma Press. 1963.

Spotted Tail's Folk, *(A History of the Brule Sioux).* Hyde, George. University of Oklahoma Press. 1961.

Sun Chief, *(the autobiography of a Hopi Indian).* Simmons, Leo W. Yale University Press. 1963.

Sun in the Sky. O'Kane, Walter. University of Oklahoma Press. 1958.

Treaty of Medicine Lodge, The. Jones, Douglas. University of Oklahoma Press. 1966.

Truth About Geronimo, The. Davis, Britton. Yale University Press. 1963.

Wooden Leg, *(Life of a Cheyenne Indian).* Marquis, Thomas. University of Nebraska Press. 1957.

Wovoka: The Indian Messiah. Bailey, Paul. Western Lore Press. 1957.

– OTHER BOOKS FROM THE AUTHOR –

The Path of Power, by Sun Bear. The life and story of Sun Bear, medicine teacher of Ojibwa descent and founder of the Bear Tribe Medicine Society. Written in his down–to–earth, humorous style, he shares his background, his visions and the path he has followed to fulfill them. Through this book, you will come to know Sun Bear, and to understand the need for the sacred teachings that he has dedicated his life to sharing with the world. Through his words, discover how to follow your own path of power, and to walk in balance on the Earth Mother. — *Over 100,000 copies sold!*
$10.95 (plus $2.00 postage and handling)

The Bear Tribe's Self–Reliance Book, by Sun Bear, Wabun, Nimi-mosha and the Tribe. A guide for everyone interested in returning to the land. It contains basic skills for re–establishing a proper relationship with the land and all beings upon it, as well as Native American and New Age philosophies, prophecies, and visions.
$10.95 (plus $2.00 postage and handling)

Walk in Balance, by Sun Bear with Crysalis Mulligan, Peter Nufer and Wabun, presents a holistic pathway to personal enrichment and health. Contains Sun Bear's philosophy of healing and happiness along with tools for creating a vital, invigorating low–stress–life. *Walk in Balance* is filled with tips on how to work with your energy blocks and anger, realistically evaluate your life situation, connect with your personal path of power and use helpful diets and natural remedies.
Resource Guides: Healing Places, Associations, People.
$10.95 (plus $2.00 postage and handling)

At Home in the Wilderness, by Sun Bear. Contains invaluable tips on woodcrafting, building temporary and permanent shelters, stalking and hunting, trapping, preparing hides, firemaking, finding wild edible plants, raising vegetables, storing food, using herbal remedies — along with many other skills.
$5.95 (plus $2.00 postage and handling)

The Medicine Wheel: Earth Astrology, by Sun Bear and Wabun. A system of Earth Astrology to help guide people not only in their daily lives, but on their life path as well. The book combines Native legends, lore and wisdom, with the vision of Sun Bear to help the reader understand his or her place on the sacred Wheel of Life.
$9.95 (plus $2.00 postage and handling)

Order from:
Bear Tribe Publishing
PO Box 9167
Spokane, WA 99209
(509) 326-6561
send $1.00 for a complete catalog

Return to Creation

by Manitonquat (Medicine Story)

Return to Creation offers a new path in the search for sustaining relationships in today's world. All of us carry within us ways of relating to each other and to the Earth that are unsatisfying. With his unique training as a traditional storyteller, tribal leader, and modern psychological counselor, Medicine Story takes a compassionate and insightful look into the roles that bind us, and the roles that could free us.

Using a Native American tribal group as his model for right relationships, Medicine Story examines contemporary social values and practices and finds them deeply wanting. He is most concerned that society routinely breaks the original, natural circle of love and trust that children have for other people and the world. He feels that the spiritual beliefs which guided traditional tribal peoples are fundamentally sound.

But he does more than contrast the modern and traditional. By combining the ancient stories of his Wampanoag ancestors with his own experiences as a husband, father, counselor and tribal leader, he invites the reader to explore with him practical ways for healing the emotional damage of childhood, strengthening the family, and developing bonds of trust between individuals.

Return to Creation is *not* a call to return to times past. It is an instruction about bringing forward into the present the wisdom of aboriginal peoples the world over. Medicine Story invites us to recreate the council circles and honor each others' words by passing the talking stick, to purify the body and spirit in the sweatlodge once again, and remake the circles of love and trust that have always been a part of the Original Instructions for all people. By transplanting these time–honored and time–proven traditional practices, we can again develop the bonds of trust that exist within the Sacred Circle.

A Survival Manual for Native & Natural People
A deeply moving and sustaining book!

"We cannot expect to recreate the conditions of ages past, and few would wish to do so. Yet the spiritual understandings of these old ways are sound, and the spiritual foundations of modern society are weak and destructive. So the question is, how can we use this knowledge which is universal, in the world which we have inherited?" — **Medicine Story**

To order send **$ 9.95** plus $2.00 postage and handling to:

Bear Tribe Publishing
PO Box 9167
Spokane, WA 99209
(509) 326–6561

 is a timely and unique publication for those interested in personal growth and relationships, environmental issues and alternative lifestyles.

A national semi-annual magazine first published in 1963 (as MANY SMOKES), **WILDFIRE** blends the best of older traditions with the newest developments in science, health, appropriate technology and self-discovery. Written for the individual seeking creative choices and constructive alternatives to many of today's challenges, **WILDFIRE** offers a variety of editorial categories:

INTERVIEWS — The thoughts, the feelings and the activities of today's leading thinkers and activists explored in depth...

SEXUALITY — What is healthy sexuality and why is it so important? Human sexuality as a vital aspect of personal development and happiness...

CHILDREN — Birthing and parenting in today's world...

SELF SUFFICIENCY — Regular columns and features on gardening, homesteading, and making your own way...

HEALTH — New developments in nutrition, health aids, herbal and natural healing techniques...

CREATIVITY — Tried and tested products, discoveries and techniques that enhance our work and lives. Original visual art, literature and poetry presented...

SPIRITUALITY — **WILDFIRE** Medicine Wheel Network touches thousands of people each year through gatherings, workshops and seminars. Guided by the Native American spiritual tradition of respect for the earth and all life, **WILDFIRE** presents the teachings of all people who accent living in balance with nature...

SUBSCRIBE TO